Cats

W9-CKY-374

4/23

# WHAT CATS WANT

THE SECRET OF HOW TO
UNDERSTAND YOUR CAT

# WHAT CATS WANT

## CLAIRE BESSANT

BARRON'S

First edition for the United States, its territories and
dependencies, and the Philippine Republic published
in 2003 by Barron's Educational Series, Inc.

First published in hardback in 2002 by John Blake
Publishing Ltd, London, England

© Text copyright Claire Bessant
Pictures reproduced by permission of Jane Burton (Warren Photographic)

All rights reserved. No part of this book may be reproduced
in any form, by photostat, microfilm, xerography, or any other
means, or incorporated into any information retrieval system,
electronic or mechanical, without the written permission
of the copyright owner.

*All inquiries should be addressed to:*
Barron's Educational Series, Inc.
250 Wireless Boulevard
Hauppauge, New York 11788
**http://www.barronseduc.com**

International Standard Book No. 0-7641-2570-2

*Library of Congress Catalog Card No. 2002114979*

Printed in China
9 8 7 6 5 4 3 2 1

# Contents

# Introduction: What Cats Want

The position of the cat as a pet in our society has changed dramatically over the past fifty to sixty years. No longer the animal that lives outside a great deal of the time and is fed a few scraps and some milk if it is lucky, the cat has moved right into the hearts of our homes, not just to the fireside but into our very beds. With this growing popularity comes a greater intimacy and a greater density of cats – and a greater need to control and protect them. They have obtained a higher emotional value and we want to have a tighter hold on them.

But do we want too much from our cats now? For thousands of years they have lived fairly independently alongside us. Now we want more control. Have we forgotten what cats are all about; are we in danger of pushing them too far? Luckily, for most of us the cat is a highly adaptable creature and is capable of maintaining two lives very successfully: exercising its wild and adult side out of doors and its kitten side within our homes. But are we trying to cut off that wild side altogether, to make it into a kitten-cat all the time?

This book tries to take a look at what makes cats what they are, and not only how that fits in with our lives but also how we are changing the rules or moving the goalposts. What do our cats want of us and how does this tie in with what we want of them? Are they stressed and, if so, what are the signs?

We know quite a bit about the behavior of our cats – I pay tribute to all the researchers whose work I have quoted in this book. They are the ones who have sat in cold parks and followed feral cats around, watched cats' reactions and interactions in different situations and patiently recorded their behaviors; they have systematically tried to understand how the cat communicates and how it sees its world. They have also looked at some of the ways we interact with our cats. I have not named many names, as I have attempted to bring together what we know without too many references, but that doesn't mean we should not be grateful for the hours, days, and years of work that have gone into gathering the information which I have drawn from in this book.

I am in a unique position to have a look at what is available. I work with veterinarians and veterinary behaviorists and have access to the science behind what we find – I also have daily contact with cat owners to understand the problems they have in the home. Some of the work, for example that concerning stress and health, is very new – we are still struggling to find the links in human medicine, let alone in our cats. But discoveries are emerging and we are learning all the time.

What we must never forget in these days of technology and fast living is that cats are still essentially the animals they were when they lived in Egypt. They have blended into our busy lives extremely smoothly, but we must never forget just what a cat is and what it needs and wants as it lives alongside us.

# The Perfect Pet

Social, vocally centered biped meets top-of-the-chain solitary scent-communicating predator. It's love at first sight for the biped and the two form a nonjealous, mature, mutually rewarding, and respectful relationship in which the predator maintains its independence (and may even be allowed to have other relationships). Sounds too good to be true – can such a mismatched relationship last? Well, not only has it lasted, it seems to be getting stronger! Man (or perhaps more often, woman) meets cat and the fascination continues. The mystery in the relationship has kept the flames burning.

In days gone past it was not wholly socially acceptable to be so smitten by an animal in such a way. The working dog was held in high regard because it had a role, and thus humanity had a reason to lavish it with attention and affection, and was not just being "soft." The cat had no real role (save that of ad hoc vermin control) and was seen as something of little value that lived alongside us rather than with us. For men especially, acknowledging affection for a cat was seen as rather odd. In the Middle Ages, women who liked cats were seen as witches and, until recently, a cat that was loved was explained away, rather condescendingly, as a "child substitute."

How times and attitudes have changed! The cat, long considered a second-class citizen to the dog in terms of a place by the fire, has quietly moved from living outside, pushed the dog out of the way, and even had the nerve to take over the master's best chair! In the United Kingdom, for example, there are more pet cats than pet dogs – 7.5 million cats compared to 6.1 million dogs. These cats live in about 5 million homes – thus, the average cat-owning home there has one-and-a-half cats. And whereas people tend to keep just one dog, many households have multiple cats (over one-fifth of people who keep dogs keep more than one, whereas over one-third of cat owners have more than one feline) – but more of this later.

It is now acceptable to heap love and sentiment on our animals – indeed, the old-fashioned and rather more structured role of the working dog, which is kept outside, is rather frowned upon by pet lovers – a pet's place is seen to be central to the family unit. Today, unless you are seen to behave lovingly to your animal, you are frowned upon! Cats have done well out of this change of attitude and, as will be discussed later, their adaptability has enabled them to take full advantage of it.

How has the cat made this transition from low-value rodent-controller to prized companion in such a relatively short period of time? Has the cat done anything different? The answer is that the cat hasn't, but that humanity has changed considerably. The cat has merely moved into the role opened up to it by our changing lifestyles and attitudes and blossomed there. What factors have contributed to this?

# THE TIME FACTOR

Our lives have never been so busy. People are working harder and longer hours; expectations of dedication to work (demonstrated by longer, unpaid working hours) have increased. Although there is a small voice of concern raised about family values and the need for time for parents to spend with their children, pressure of work usually means that people stay there long after official office hours. Those working for themselves also have to put in long hours to ensure they take up all opportunities and are available to the people who are still in their offices! It's a vicious circle. Indeed, far from living with a shorter working week with time for hobbies – as predicted twenty years ago – today our working lives are characterized by the need to prove our dedication and to give up more of our free time.

Thirty to forty years ago there was also a dramatic difference in the home – women still usually stayed home to care for husband, children, and house in whichever combination they occurred. Today, both partners in a relationship usually work, simply to pay for mortgages and the other expenses of life. Child care responsibilities have to be fitted in between work and other commitments, leaving little free time. However, being at home does allow a person to organize those dull chores, such as cleaning the house, shopping, doing laundry, and paying the bills. These days such things have to be done late at night or on the weekend, and most of the latter can be taken up by domestic duties or children's activities. There is little time to relax and little time for any unorganized activity; simply chilling out has become a luxury option. The cat requires little formal time – e.g., for walking – and so can be opportunistic and snatch small bits of our time here and there.

# THE RESPONSIBILITY FACTOR

Mankind's traditional best friend, the dog, is having a hard time fitting into our busy schedules. As a pack animal, its instincts cry out for it to be part of a group, where it feels more secure. It can be stressed by being left alone all day and this may lead it to embark on destructive activity. Because we are legally responsible for our dogs' activities, we also have to know where they are and have control over them all the time: an uncontrolled dog can be a nuisance and, at worst, a danger to the public. Even a controlled dog can dirty the pavement or cause noise pollution by barking all day in a house or yard. Thus, there is great pressure on owners to provide an environment in which the dog is happy and to ensure that it is well behaved and safe around other people and animals. In the countryside, a loose dog can do great damage to livestock. Dogs seldom come to us perfectly trained or behaved – like children, they need time and some expertise to be taught what is acceptable and what is not; how to fit into the group around them. They also need access to exercise areas.

We are legally responsible for the behavior of our dogs. If they cause harm or damage we may have to pay the consequences. We are not responsible for our cats' mischief – if a cat were to break into a pigeon loft and kill some of the birds there, it would be up to the owner of the loft to build it more strongly to prevent the cat getting in. Sometimes this can work against the cat. In some regions, if you hit a dog while driving your car, you are legally required to report the incident – not so with a cat. Under some laws, a dog should not be out on its own and in our cities and towns. Animal control workers ensure that any dog found wandering is taken off the streets. Thus, while a cat may be seen as less important in the eyes of the law, this means that less control is required and there is less onus on owners to control their cats.

# THE NURTURE FACTOR

The number of people who have the time, space, and knowledge to keep a dog is decreasing. Yet, whatever it is that makes us like to keep pets – perhaps we might call it the "nurture factor" – has not disappeared. We like to care for something; we like to be welcomed home by something that in turn responds to us unconditionally. It is not pleasant to go home after a long day in the office to an empty house. Being met by a pet that is delighted to see you and welcome you gives you a lift. Enter the cat – clean, independent, unlikely to get lonely, good on companionship, and low on maintenance – the answer to our prayers. Moreover, it is unlikely to cause our neighbors and friends much (if any) nuisance or danger.

# THE COMPANIONSHIP FACTOR

Cats make excellent companions. Most are happy to mooch around the house with their owners, taking a nap on or near them, and generally joining in by sitting on the newspaper that someone is attempting to read, filling the computer with hairs as they lounge on top, or puttering around with us in the garden. Stroking a purring cat can be wonderfully relaxing and great therapy.

There have been many studies on the benefits of dog ownership – dog owners have lower blood pressure, less depression, and recover from illness more quickly than those without canine companions. Some of this may be due to the exercise that is part and parcel of owning a dog – and which, of course, is missing from this list of feline factors. Cat owners are spared the need to go out in all kinds of weather and pound the pavement and can look forward to a warm cuddle in front of the fire instead of a cold excursion in the winter. Admittedly, they do miss out on the contact with strangers that usually accompanies a walk with a dog – all sorts of people stop and talk to you, feeling they can approach and make conversation if it starts with a comment to or about the dog. There are even schemes in practice whereby owners of temperament-tested dogs are taken into hospitals and homes to visit the patients; undoubtedly some people obtain great therapeutic benefit from meeting and petting dogs. There is a similar scheme for cats, but it does take a rather special cat to enjoy going off its own territory and meeting strangers in a strange place. Cats usually want to take their time to assess a person and decide if they want to make contact. Cat companionship is of a rather more personal nature than the sociable companionship characteristic of many dogs.

## THE FEMALE FACTOR

Women's role in our society has changed even more rapidly than that of cats! Women now juggle home and work and are equal decision makers within the home. The male-orientated household, in which the man would probably have chosen a pet to fit the perhaps more male role of the dog, is vanishing rapidly. For whatever reason, women like cats. Moreover, they are "allowed" to like cats and to form strong relationships with them, and tend to choose them in preference to the dog – one possible major reason for this being that cats are easier to keep.

## THE ONE-TO-ONE FACTOR

But it is not only women who like cats. Men have had a hard time being allowed to say they love their cats and often, men prefer the more controllable, nonquestioning loyalty and obedience of the dog. And perhaps because they have not owned a cat, their assumptions about the cats are based on viewing at a distance – the cat may seem independent and aloof; it will probably not run up to strangers and ask for attention the way a dog will, and thus close encounters with cats may have been few and far between. However, the convert, as is often the case, can be the strongest advocate of the cat. Many self-confessed male canine lovers might never have chosen to take on a cat, but for some reason a cat may have come into their lives, either accidentally or because it arrived with a new partner or via a child. They may initially view the cat as nonloyal and rather too independent, but will usually find themselves gradually won over by its intelligence, its grace, and that same feeling of "specialness" we all get when the cat runs to greet us or deems to grace us as its choice of soft lap. These men are the first to become distressed if the cat is ill, and the most upset when it is lost.

They also get to study the cat in comparison to the dog and, quite frankly, the cat often makes the dog look rather a fool, falling over itself to please its owner or hanging around waiting for a word or pat. The cat seems immensely cool, calm, and collected seen alongside its canine cousin. Indeed in the cat/dog relationship, it is usually the cat that is in charge. Many times a cat will simply sit and stare at a dog, which will not catch its eye, and will sit or even lie down to try and avoid the feline attention! Of course, some cats and dogs become the best of friends – the lack of inter-species competition allows them to enjoy each other without fear of losing position!

## THE GUILT FACTOR

Guilt provides another strong reason for the popularity of cats. These days people have many demands on their time – they can't manage to do everything, and feel guilty about those things they cannot fit in.

One's partner does not get enough of one's time; one's children do not even get that "quality" time which is supposed to be allotted to them and thus make parents feel better and, to crown it all, the dog is unhappy because it doesn't receive enough attention – more guilt. A dog that has been left alone too long may soil in the house, howl, bark, or chew up the furniture because it feels distressed at being left alone. Such behavior not only causes dog owners to worry about annoying the neighbors, but makes owners feel very guilty about leaving the dog alone for too long.

The cat, on the other hand, is more often than not very happy to be left alone and will get on with its own life without too much worry. Because cats will usually eat in a fairly measured fashion, they can be left food to eat as they wish; they can go outside if they need to or be provided with a litter tray and thus are not crossing their legs if their owner is stuck on the highway outside of town for two hours. Cats are content without too much input. An owner can alleviate any small worry that they might get lonely by getting two kittens together so they have company when they are left alone. Two cats are seldom much more work than one and they provide at least twice the fun.

## THE HOUSE-PROUD FACTOR

Because people are working longer hours and money is perhaps not as readily available as it was in the late '80s and early '90s, we do not actually have a great deal of free time. Our entertainment is often centered around the house – home entertainment centers with large-screen TVs, DVDs, videos, and satellite dishes are all aimed at those who don't go out all the time, but have home-based entertainment or relaxation. Our televisions have been swamped by a glut of home design programs over the past few years and, as a consequence, we are all much more interested in what our rooms look like and how to get the best from them. One such program, *House Doctor*, which features a female Californian house expert who will give a house a makeover in order to help it to sell, has majored on this lady's frankness about the fact that dogs make a house smell and can thus make finding a buyer problematic. Even the cleanest and youngest of dogs can smell pretty bad if it gets wet – and the older and damper the dog, the worse the situation becomes. While country dog owners may have a mud room or an outdoor kennel for the dog, at least until it dries out, most homes have to contend with a damp dog in the kitchen, and wiping up the muddy paw prints and wiping down the mud spatters all over the walls. Cats do leave hairs around and if you have a very fluffy type of cat, this can be a problem. Thankfully cats don't smell (unless you don't clean out the litter tray regularly). They also look great draped over the new throw on the couch, or lying on the area rug.

## THE FELINE FACTOR

Even the scruffiest battle-worn tomcat has a certain grace – but the healthy, young, supple cat has an elegant beauty of form and movement that is hard to beat. Luckily we have not tried, or have not been able if we have tried, to change the feline form too much. Some pedigree cats may vary in how much hair they have, or in their body form from slim to more stocky in shape, but the feline form, the beautiful eye color, coat color or pattern, and the fluidity of movement and grace remain. It is a joy to have such beauty in our homes.

## THE CAT-FLAP FACTOR

The cat flap is second only to the litter tray in making cat-keeping easy. It removes the need to control or be at the beck and call of our cats; they can be in or out as they please without needing a middle man. Modern cat flaps do allow us some control if we want it – to shut out the world, or to keep cats in at night, or during potentially stressful occasions, such as firework displays. Sometimes flaps can make it all too easy to let any cat in the neighborhood visit, but in terms of boosting the popularity of cats as pets, it has had a great effect.

## THE COST FACTOR

For most people, obtaining a cat costs very little. Only about 10 percent of cats in homes are pedigree cats and have a purchase cost associated with them – usually several hundred dollars. The remaining owners obtain their cats from a variety of sources, from going to a rescue shelter, to taking on a kitten from a friend's cat, or simply having one turn up on the doorstep. In many cases cats cost little or nothing to acquire. Kittens are often "free to a good home" from people who have not realized that their kitten is no longer a kitten – the local tom knows immediately of course, but by the time the owners notice, it is too late!

However, whether you have a mixed breed or a pedigree, the cost of keeping it is the same – vaccinations, worm and flea treatment, insurance, food, and litter – all cats have the same requirements and this is not an insubstantial cost.

## THE AGE FACTOR

The cat is also a long-lived pet. In general, the larger the animal, the longer it lives – mice live shorter lives than rabbits and dogs outlive rabbits. However, in general, cats will outlive dogs. Interestingly, within the different pedigree dog breeds, the reverse is usually the norm – the bigger the breed, the shorter the life. This has probably more to do with the extremes we have gone to in breeding than what would naturally happen if dogs were allowed to breed together to form that medium-sized black-and-brown mongrel we still see from time to time. Within dogs, too, the more active breeds usually live longer – the Jack Russell and the collie being particularly well known for their longevity. The average age for a dog is probably about 12 years; for cats it is thought to be about 14 years. Anecdotally, some breeds are said to live longer than others – the Siamese and Burmese often live into their late teens or twenties. Perhaps it is because cats are active animals, or because they know how to relax when they are not being active. Whatever the reason, it means they are with us for a long time – sometimes as long as our children – and become very special companions in our lives.

## THE ACCEPTANCE FACTOR

We do not feel the need to change our cat's behavior to fit in with what society expects; in contrast, we tend to feel a responsibility to ensure that our dogs behave in a socially acceptable way. Our relationship with cats is rather different and we are usually very happy for them to have their own very different personalities and even accept behavior that may not please. This also makes the cat easy on the conscience, as we don't feel we have to be watching out for it all the time.

## THE CAT – A PERFECT PET

To sum it up in a couple of sentences: the cat is a clever, beautiful animal that provides great companionship while retaining an independent and graceful self-respect that makes us feel honored to be with it. Aside from that, it is clean, quiet, and doesn't hurt anyone. What more could we want?

Thus, through no effort of its own, aside from behaving as it always has, the cat has found itself fitting a role for which it has not actually even auditioned. We are the makers of the cat-shaped hole – the cat, with its great adaptability, has happily settled in.

# How It All Began

To consider what comes later in the book in terms of what cats need or want, it is very useful to understand how the cat has come to be in this position alongside humanity – after all, why not a ferret or a racoon? How has the cat become "domesticated"?

## HOW IT ALL BEGAN ...

About 4,000 years ago, the ancient Egyptians – a strong and inventive race – began to store grain; these stores enabled the Egyptians to spread their harvest throughout the year. Of course, the availability of grain also attracted animals such as rats and mice, which also benefited from this year-round availability of food. No doubt they ate and bred very successfully. Luckily for the Egyptians, there were predators that fed on these rodents and kept the numbers down. Among these were North African wildcats – a breed of sandy-colored cats with some darker striped markings on their legs and

13

tails. They would have been slightly larger than our domestic cats and no doubt initially very timid.

Researchers believe that we are lucky that the African wildcat (*Felis silvestris lybica*) seemed to be able to get over its shyness and start to live close to mankind. An abundance of prey would have meant that the wildcats could feed and stay healthy and thus reproduce successfully. Perhaps the Egyptians started to capture some of the kittens and bring them up in or near their homes – the kittens must have been (like all kittens) very appealing. The Egyptians had many generations to play with – they could choose the friendliest or the prettiest and keep them – inevitably these would have bred and been kept close to hand. The European wildcat, even if hand-reared or handled at an early age, will revert to its wild behavior as it grows – it is highly sensitive to danger and reacts quickly – ensuring it will survive to live another day. It may be, therefore, that the African wildcat had certain genetic traits that allowed it the possibility of adapting to domesticity.

Research has revealed that during this time of "domestication" the cat's brain became smaller. The areas of cats' brains that kept them "jumpy" – those areas sensitive to sound and movement – are actually smaller today. This makes evolutionary sense: for cats to live with humans they have to become willing to stay with us while we crash and bang around as we go about our daily lives. The calmer cats would have been able to do this. Indeed, the size of the cats' adrenal glands have also reduced over the millennia. The adrenal glands produce the hormone adrenaline – the hormone responsible for what we call the "fight or flight" response. Less adrenaline would mean that cats were not so reactive and so less likely to run away.

Those cats that started to live closer to the Egyptians not only had to overcome a fear of man and all the activities that go on in a town or city, but also to be able to live close to other cats. Wildcats are usually strongly territorial and live very solitary lives, only coming together with other cats for mating. After the young are reared, they move on and the parent cats live alone again. The reasons for this are probably based on availability of food. A female would have an area from which she could gain enough food to survive herself and, during the breeding season, feed a litter of kittens. Another cat in the area would severely reduce her chance of success. By making use of the abundance of food around the Egyptian settlements, the restrictions on food availability were removed – cats could live closer together if they were able to adapt to this type of behavior and not automatically maintain exclusive territories. Again, the cats that were able to do this would have benefited from the food availability.

To sum up, during this period cats became more friendly toward man; they became physically smaller; their brains became smaller, and they became less reactive. Other changes in the appearance of cats may have begun with their domestication in ancient Egypt. The original African wildcat has an agouti coat – like a wild rabbit's coat, it is made of hairs that have stripes of different colors across them – ideal for camouflage. Having begun to keep cats, did the Egyptians then start to breed from those with slightly different coat patterns or mutations in color which arose, to breed cats for an aesthetically attractive appearance?

## "DOMESTICATED"?

We may marvel at the ability of the African wildcat to adapt and be adapted by humanity to "domestication," but despite this huge change to its lifestyle and reactivity, the cat has remained relatively unchanged by mankind. Unlike cattle or sheep, which can be said to be fully domesticated, the cat has walked a thin line between domesticity and wildness – perhaps it can be said to have met us halfway to domestication. Our pet cat, *Felis catus*, still retains the ability to live a completely feral lifestyle if it wants to, or has to – the biological independence to live with us or without us and survive.

Let us look for a moment at that other animal we have domesticated as a pet: the dog. Humanity has been able to take the dog and breed it for a multitude of different tasks, including companionship, retrieval, fighting, running, or hunting. Along with the requirement for the task came changes in body size and shape that enabled the dog to undertake whichever task was required – a small body for going down rabbit holes or a large muscular body for protection or fighting; a lithe, agile body for running miles and herding sheep, or long legs and a lightweight body for running fast. With the body changes came changes in temperament. However, any developments had to allow for the fact that the dog must live peacefully with man without causing danger to him or his family. Thus, the dog has been changed and molded to fit human requirements – it ranges in size from the tiny Chihuahua to the huge mastiff or Irish wolfhound.

We haven't been able to do the same for cats – or perhaps we just haven't tried because we have not been able to make cats do our bidding. They have been genetically adaptable enough to change from wildcat to domesticated cat, from *Felis sylvestris* to *Felis catus*, but there adaptability has ended. Man has been able to experiment with the genes for coat color and length and to some extent for body shape – consider our breeds of snub-nosed, long-haired Persian with a stocky body compared to the slim, long-legged, quite fragile-looking

Siamese. These are quite different, but still roughly the same size and exhibit basically the same behavior. They do not show the wide variation in behavior seen between, say, a Labrador and a terrier, or a Greyhound and a King Charles Spaniel.

Thus, the cat has been able to make the best of its association with man while maintaining much of its self-sufficiency and physically changing very little.

# The Natural Cat

To set the scene against which to look at our pet cat in our homes and living according to our lifestyles, we need first to look at the natural cat – how it behaves and the ways in which it interacts with its environment without people. In order to see how we fit in with the cat we need to look at what motivates cats and how they behave without the benefit of human helpers. How do they interact with other cats, how do they like to live, and what do they avoid? To do this we need to look at the behavior of feral cats or wild-living domestic cats. At this point it is worth taking time to define the different terms we use when we talk about the different guises of *Felis catus* when it associates with man.

**Feral cats** are domestic cats gone wild. True ferals will act like wild animals – they will not accept handling and will be terrified if trapped. They can live alongside humans and scavenge available food, but adult ferals will seldom, if ever, make happy, confident pets – they should be respected as wild animals.

**Semi-feral cats** are cats that have probably had some contact with people previously; perhaps they were strays that have grouped together around a food source or have joined other true ferals. Many may be tameable and, if they receive particular attention, may be happy to become house cats again.

**Farm cats** could probably be grouped with ferals or semi-ferals. However, we have long given them a grouping of their own. They are as we imagine cats to have been – drinking milk off the doorstep, in the parlor, and chasing rats around the farmyard. Of course, times have changed and soft brown cows don't spend too much time these days in wooden barns chewing contentedly with shafts of sun shining through the broken slats while the farm cats play in the warm straw. However, there are still many cats on farms and they do help to keep rodents at bay around grain silos. They live alongside the farm inhabitants and may be fed or even come into the house; however, they often live independently from humans, although they will be familiar, and may even be friendly, with the people there.

**Pet cats** are familiar to all of us and we expect to live with a cat that will enjoy sharing our lives and will choose to stay with us in our homes. The cat will probably have a relatively free existence and be able to come and go as it pleases. We consider the pet cat to be part of the family and will take it with us if we move, put it in a kennel when we go on vacation and care for it if it is sick. However, should most cats have to, they could survive in a semi-feral state.

There are a couple of subcategories of pet cats that differ from the "original" pet cat in the way they are kept and what they are capable of doing. Some cats are now kept totally indoors because their owners cannot or will not let them out. These indoor cats, almost by definition, have a closer relationship with their owners because they are dependent on them for everything – food, toilet facilities, and entertainment. If they were to get outside, they might panic initially, but would adapt quite quickly.

Among the pedigree cats there are several breeds that may not do so well if they had to live the wild life. The pedigree Persian has been bred with such a thick, long undercoat that it cannot actually groom itself adequately. If its owners do not groom it regularly, the coat will become matted and form clumps that the meticulous cat would probably find most uncomfortable and stressful. The Persian also has a very flat face, which may make it difficult for the cat to groom and hunt to kill, so it might not fare well if it had to return to a wild existence. Likewise, the hairless Sphynx might not survive a harsh winter if it is forced to fend for itself.

## LIVING TOGETHER

In order to understand our cats, it would be useful first of all to look at how cats live together. Changes in their ancestors allowed cats to live more closely together. How far have those changes gone in our pet cats?

The European wildcat – a wild felid that likes to keep itself to itself and has a territory to match – may live in densities of between one and three cats per square mile. However, groups of cats that live around a source of food, such as a garbage dump, or a dock, or hotel, or who are regular feeders, may reach a density of 100 cats per square mile. On farms where they are also fed, cats can live at densities of 5 to 100 per square mile. In city areas they have been known to have a density of as many as 2,000 per square mile.

In a group of feral cats, the density of cats in a certain area may also be affected by the availability of shelter – certainly it is the female cats that form the basis of these groups and they will need some form of den or hidden hole in which to bring up their young. Female territories thus depend on food and shelter. Male territories depend on females!

The range of female cats is determined by food abundance and distribution – they need just enough space to give them access to food all year round and to raise their kittens. Variation in the size of the female territory will depend on whether this food is concentrated in one place or is spread over a large area.

The range of breeding males is about three times that of females – it changes throughout the year, depending on where the breeding females are and on the time of year. Nonbreeding males have a smaller territory – probably about the same as that of females.

If females have to live on natural prey, they usually have a solitary lifestyle – there is only enough food available to allow one cat to live and reproduce. However, if there is a source of food, such as a garbage dump or trash cans nearby, then groups of cats can live quite closely together. Usually these groups are comprised of related female cats and their offspring. Recently born female kittens may stay around while young males are pushed out to move on elsewhere. These younger males may not breed for several years – the large, fiercer breeding males will not allow this. Breeding males will move between groups of females. Unlike lions, the males do not seem to form bands of brothers, but stick to a fairly solitary lifestyle.

How did the African wildcat ancestor of our domestic cat overcome its strong instincts of being solitary and come to live in groups? The theory is that as long as the food source is good enough and is situated in one area, then cats can start to come together. Indeed, they can now be so close that females will share the care of kittens and defend their den together – cooperative defense of kittens will benefit them all. Perhaps this is why the females that do group together are related: there is benefit in supporting all the kittens because they have similar genes and are therefore worth protecting. Females from outside the group will be chased off. Males are sent away and only a few will reach breeding status. Strange males, however, will be accepted more readily than strange females. This is understandable, as new females will compete for food and shelter.

Male territories actually overlap each other; they cannot defend a huge area all the time. Most breeding males adopt a roaming mating tactic between groups or solitary females. The same pattern is seen in wild felids. Breeding males roam more than subordinate males. Thus, group living depends on human help – food availability in large areas – and stable groups based on related females.

## GROUP LIVING

Let's look a little more closely at these feline groups. Even solitary-living wild female felines will actually spend about 80 percent of their time in a group – of their own making – with their kittens. To reiterate:

Domestic cats will form groups if there is enough food around – groups consist of related females and generations of their female kittens. These will be aggressive to any other female cats which are not related to them. Breeding males will come and go from group to group and young male kittens will be driven off to wander into their own territories. Unlike lions, they do not seem to join up and form gangs of young males, but go their own solitary ways. The breeding males have little contact with kittens and will be hostile and aggressive to other adult males – if the group is small they will also be aggressive to juvenile males, perhaps because they are more of a threat in a small group. Female cats may give birth together and share the suckling and care of kittens.

Researchers have studied many groups of cats and have found that male kittens have stronger interactions with their male littermates than with older male kittens. Likewise, female kittens seem to prefer their littermates to their older sisters. Is this to do with the fact that they have been with them during the socialization period and so have stronger bonds?

# COMMUNICATING

By looking at the way cats leave signals for each other and communicate by various means in different situations, we can perhaps understand some of the signals they leave for us. We may also be able to unravel the reasons for some of their behavioral patterns, especially those which we may see as problems (such as indoor spraying) by ascertaining the circumstances in which these behaviors occur in the wild-living cat.

In the way they communicate, our domestic cats can once again be compared to their solitary-living feline cousins. They also need separate consideration because they live at much greater densities than these wildcats and can choose to live in groups (like lions), albeit without the hunting cooperation. Thus, they communicate not just with long-distance signals, but at much closer range and have perhaps developed ways of doing this that are absent in their wilder relatives.

When animals live closely to one another they have to learn to tolerate each other and have some way of communicating to avoid conflict and thus, injury. Dogs are pack-living animals – they need a pack around them to feel secure and have a behavioral repertoire that allows them to fit into a slot within the pack and to appease, submit, or dominate as befitting their status or place in the pack (or desired place in the pack). Thus, although there may be a great deal of grumbling or cringing going on, there is little outright aggression and the pack works well together. For this, dogs have the ability to perform a wide range of body language in order to work together and prevent injury. Dog groups do have a hierarchy, and the rules of status prevent them from hurting each other unnecessarily and save energy by having a structure whereby the group knows how to act and doesn't need to make an issue out of each decision.

The only group-living cats that cooperate during hunting are lions; they also live in groups and manage to live seemingly in harmony. However, these are female groups with cubs. The male lives alongside the females until it is ousted by a younger or fitter rival; males do not have to live alongside each other in harmony. Young males will form small groups when they are of an age to be pushed out of the pride.

Our domestic cats fit into both these camps and have a variety of signals that help them to communicate with other cats.

For the solitary-living cat, most communication is directed at keeping other cats away – scent messages can be left that will last for several hours or even days, although the endurance and success of the signal may depend on the weather not washing it away or blowing it in the wrong direction. Another problem that can occur is that circumstances may change more quickly than the message. It's a bit like sending a letter second class to say you will be in on a certain date: during the time it takes to get to its destination you find that something urgent has come up and you will need to change the instructions – thank goodness for the phone or e-mail to override the original message. For wild, solitary-living cats it may not be easy to change the message quickly.

As we have seen, the level of food available will often be the deciding factor as to whether cats live solitary lives or in groups. Cats will defend their territories and try to push away other cats so they do not put added pressure on food resources, or take over precious shelters where cats can keep their kittens safely. Males, too, will repel other males. However, defense is not necessarily the same as out-and-out war – male cats can fight very fiercely and have the weapons to cause great damage. That said, they will have gone through a large number of signals and threats before a confrontation finally takes place. There are many opportunities to back down – cats don't submit in the way dogs do, but they can remove themselves from the conflict situation. If you can manage to scare off your opponent, you do not have to risk physical injury, which can be fatal if wounds become infected. Cats do not have the social stratification of the dog in terms of dominance and submission in order to fit in with a group that must work as a whole for hunting and group living. In the feline world, peace is maintained by threat and compromise, not for the benefit of a group, but for the good of the individual. Group living also adds complications – not only do individuals have a personal scent, but members of a group will have a group scent that marks them as part of the team. Cats without this marker are considered outsiders. Cats could be termed nonobligatory social animals and can interact in a friendly way if they want to. They do not live in organized groups – some cats may be more intolerant, oppressive, or domineering than others, but it is not an organized agreement that all the cats have accepted.

There are, of course, circumstances when even the most solitary of animals wants to make contact and this is vital to the survival of the species. In this case, the message in the signal changes and male cats will soon track down a female in estrus (heat) that wants to be found.

Cats use several methods of long-distance communication to let other cats know about their reproductive state or to tell them to keep away. They use urine and feces as well as glandular secretions from various other parts of the body that not only reassure them in their own territory, but tell other cats about their presence. Loud vocal communications that carry over distance are only made during times when males and females want to get together or when males are keeping other males from getting to the females they wish to get to! The calling of the female in season and the caterwauling of the male carry over a long distance. Most other vocal communication is also aimed at keeping other cats away and is used in much closer quarters in conjunction with body language – the communication between queens (mother cats) and their kittens being an exception. Close-quarter communication is also extremely scent-based for the cat and is used in combination with body language.

## LONG-DISTANCE COMMUNICATION

Cats are equipped with an excellent sense of smell and can even concentrate scents by drawing air into a special organ in the roof of the mouth called Jacobson's organ – the grimacing look on the cat's face (in which it raises its upper lip and holds its mouth slightly open) is called the Flehmen response and can also be seen in horses and deer. With specific movements of its lip and tongue the cat pushes the air into the organ in a series of short breaths. This allows cats to concentrate the molecules in the air inside the organ and get much more information about it. In this way cats move in a world rich in scents from which they constantly glean information.

Among many creatures, from insects to mammals, there is a means of communication whereby a chemical (called a pheromone) produced by one animal will trigger a reaction in another. The term pheromone comes from the Greek "pheros," meaning "far," and "horman," meaning "to excite." Tiny amounts of these pheromones will elicit a certain behavior from a distance in animals of the same species. Pheromones have a role in sexual communication and it is in this aspect that we often see our cats reacting to them. If you watch a male cat in the garden after another cat has been through, you will notice that he samples the areas that the cat has marked or sprayed and often you will see the characteristic Flehmen response – if the mark has been left by a female cat in season, then the response will be marked. We think of the scents left by the cat from glands on its face, paws, back, and tail areas as pheromones.

Urine can be used most effectively as a long-distance message – indeed, we believe that the reason most cats will dig a hole and cover the urine they deposit is to try and not leave a message that they are there. If a queen has kittens nearby, she doesn't want other predators hanging around waiting to make a meal of them. By covering the urine, scents are contained in the soil and prevented from escaping into the air, thereby preventing others from knowing there are cats around. This may work very well for solitary cats where territories are large and the smell of the urine stands a good chance of decomposing in the ground without being discovered by another animal. However, for our pet cats, which live very closely with others, it may not be very successful.

Urine can also be used as a red flag in terms of catching attention.

Instead of squatting to bury and hide the scent, cats can deposit urine on to a vertical surface at cat-face height, leaving it to blow further afield. To deposit the urine in this way – i.e., to spray it backwards – cats take up a standing position and paddle their back feet up and down while quivering their tail. A small volume of urine is squirted backwards. Toms spray most frequently and even more frequently if there is a female in season in the vicinity.

Added to urine are secretions from the anal glands and as the urine degrades and bacteria start to break it down, it produces that exceptionally strong scent of tomcat urine which is so distinctive and can't be missed. It seems that the spray contains amino acids that are degraded by the bacteria to produce sulphide containing compounds which are distinctive to tomcat spray. Apparently, the smelliness of the spray may be an indication of the male's health. In order to produce lots of these amino acids that degrade to produce the smell, the cat must have ingested plenty in the first place from a good diet – i.e., the cat is likely to be strong and healthy if its urine is good and smelly! On a still day, tomcat urine can be detected by another cat from more than 40 feet (12 m) away.

Researchers and observers of feline behavior are unsure whether cats use feces as a means of leaving a message or not. Most cats in their own territory will dig a hole, deposit the feces and cover it up; we are still unsure as to whether it does so to mask the scents it holds or perhaps just as good housekeeping to ensure the health of their core area. However, many carnivores do leave feces in prominent places (a habit known as "middening") as a message of some sort to others. Cats can do this too.

Cats may also leave scratches and scent marks along pathways they regularly use. These scents are a way of organizing the cat's territory –

they are termed spacing pheromones and they aim to let other cats know where the no-go core areas are and where there can be some sharing of walkways. The scratches help mark the area with a visual signal should the pheromones become washed away.

Aside from this, long-distance signals will include those which can be heard over a distance – these are the sounds produced between cats trying to attract each other, such as the calling of the female in season, or caterwauling of tomcats letting the females know they are around and keeping each other at bay while in pursuit of females. These are all known as "strained intensity sounds" produced when the cat is ready for mating or fighting in what we might term an emotionally charged state.

In summary, most long-distance signals are aimed at keeping other cats away unless it is time for mating, during which females will call loudly and repeatedly for males to come to them.

## COMMUNICATING AT CLOSE QUARTERS

For wild cats that have solitary lifestyles, long-distance communications are used for most of their interactions with other adult animals, save for mating. Obviously, there is close communication with kittens. Our pet cats, like lions, can also be group-living animals and have a repertoire of scent and visual signals that allows them to let other cats know what they want. Vocal communications are seldom used, except with kittens (and, of course, with people – but more of that later).

Scratching or clawing, usually carried out on vertical wooden posts or trees, seems to have three roles for cats: It pulls the old blunt covering layer off the nail, revealing a sharp new point underneath; it leaves a visual signal of the cat's presence; and it leaves a scent message with secretions from the glands between the pads on the underside of the paw. Cats that are "dominant" or feel themselves to be of a higher ranking than other cats will scratch in the presence of the latter – again, perhaps as a sign of which cat wants to control the area.

Scents also play a large role in close-quarter communication. The cat has various glands on its skin that produce secretions personal to that cat. These are situated under the chin, at the corners of the mouth, on the temples either side of the forehead, at the base of the tail, and along the tail.

Cats will rub these areas on twigs and vertical objects to leave messages perhaps for themselves and for other cats. Although we can see and smell nothing, other cats will be very interested in these spots when "bunting" (the rubbing of scent) has taken place. Tomcats will be very interested in the scents left by female cats in season, so this type of information must be conveyed by the scents.

Cats also rub each other and exchange odors, giving them an individual odor to which is attached a group smell comprising them and the other members. The head will smell more of the individual, with the tail and sides having more of the group's scent.

Interestingly, such facial scents are thought to be left for the benefit of the cat itself – scientists have termed them familiarization pheromones. The theory is that the cat will go from area to area which it has marked in this way and the pheromones will mean something to that particular cat and make it feel secure and relaxed in that place.

Most of the cat's visual communication is, by definition, at fairly close quarters, because other cats need to see it. Thus, if they do get this close, many will be signals of conflict – cats with hair raised and standing sideways to make themselves appear larger, other cats crouched down with ears flattened to convey withdrawal and nonprovocation, and so on. How much of this is bluff and what subtle signals are moving between cats in conflict are issues that are lost on us.

It would be interesting to see if there were any types of interaction or communication, or what scientists call "signals," which group-living cats such as our domestic cat use in comparison to solitary-living cats (which our cats can be, too) which only come into visual and tactile communication with other cats for mating and, of course, during the rearing of kittens. In the excellent new version of Turner and Bateson's book *The Domestic Cat: The Biology of its Behaviour*, the authors bring together all the scientific work that has been done in this area to try and ascertain if "domestication" of our *Felis catus* has made it behave differently. It is a fascinating read for anybody interested in research into feline behavior.

That body posture we cat owners like so much – the "tail-up" approach – is, it seems, only to be seen in our pet cats and in lions, not in those species of cats with solitary existences. In other wild cats, the tail-up posture is only seen when they are spraying urine. Thus, perhaps it is some form of communication to tell other cats that this is a friendly approach – something only necessary for cats living in a group situation and aimed at avoiding conflict when approaching. Another behavioral trait seen in both our domestic cats and lions is the act of rubbing against one another. Often in this situation the cat doing the rubbing seems to be wanting to placate the one on the receiving end of the attention.

Allogrooming – a term used to describe cats grooming each other – is usually interpreted by us as a sign of affection, but it may not actually be so. Researchers have found more assertive cats groom less assertive cats and the act often ends in some form of aggression – the groomer may turn the lick into a bite! Perhaps it has a much more sinister purpose, and is a way of one cat asserting itself over the other.

Other body language, such as rolling, can be a sexual come-on from females of most species of wild cats, but it does not seem to have been recorded between males as well. In our domestic cats it is usually seen when an immature male rolls in front of a mature one – perhaps in some form of submission – again, something developed to cut down aggression where there are groups of cats living together. Rubbing of the body and cats grooming each other is almost exclusively a sexual behavior in wild felids; in our domesticated cats it is also a greeting although, interestingly, rubbing can develop in solitary cats that are kept in groups in zoos, so perhaps solitary-living cats just don't have the time together as adults to develop trusting relationships that can result in rubbing.

Thus, our domestic cats, although descended from solitary-living cats, have adapted to be able to live in groups, if there is enough food and shelter. They use plenty of long-distance signals, but also have a repertoire of communication signals that they can also use at closer quarters and which may have developed from living in groups around a source of food. We can learn from this that although they are descendants of wild cats that had very little interaction with other cats, today's domestic cats have adapted to be able to live with other cats if they wish or need to.

# 4

# What Makes a Cat?

People find cats visually pleasing and this may have been the initial impetus for the Egyptians to take them into their homes and speed up the "domestication" process. They may have taken the pretty ones, perhaps those with stronger tabby stripes on their legs or a lighter coat, and kept them together, producing kittens with slightly new or stronger coat patterns. As cats lived alongside man and mutations in color arose and were incorporated, a range of coat colors and patterns would have developed. Of course, we are still working on this process with our pedigree cats and are still developing new colors and patterns. While we have changed coat length and color, the cats are still fundamentally the same shape and size as their ancestors – there are breed differences, but individual differences still span these too and the degree of difference in size between the largest and the smallest would be only slightly over a factor of one. This may be because we have only been concentrating on breeding cats actively for about 100 years or because the cat is less amenable to change when compared to, say, the dog, which has been bred into a range of sizes and shapes which vary much more considerably – from smallest to largest is most likely several inches. Most of these changes have accompanied a change in function – for example, some dogs have been bred to run, while others may have been bred to go down holes or to scare off wolves.

Most of the cat's genes are responsible for its exceptional physiology; only a few of its genes account for its coat color or length. Our relationship with cats began because of their vermin-killing ability, but the importance of this has diminished to almost nothing (indeed now it is often seen as a negative part of the cat's behavior) while other aspects of the relationship have developed further.

We have not tried to change what a cat does and so have not altered its looks greatly. We have also not altered its behavior a great deal and across the breeds one cat is still very much the same as any other in terms of its instincts and abilities. In contrast, a Labrador is compelled to retrieve everything in the house at all times and a terrier is on the hunt for anything that moves; the cat is the same the world over and very similar in most ways to its wild ancestor *Felis silvestris lybica*.

## THE PERFECT DESIGN?

If looks are linked to function, what does a cat do to have warranted its present form? I began to think of how a group of specialist designers would pool their expertise and put together a machine to do what a cat does, and it really made me think of how amazingly clever the feline machine is. So what would be the specification that Team Feline would have to achieve?

All animals must be able to survive – to find enough food to get through the year and to reproduce and raise offspring to a stage at which they can carry on the process themselves.

For the cat specifically there are more clues as to where to start. The cat is an obligate carnivore – it must have meat in its diet to survive, because it cannot synthesize or detoxify certain chemicals that other animals can use to their benefit. It cannot survive vegetable matter – thus, there is a necessity for hunting trips to be very successful. The cat uses top-quality fuel, but must be able to refuel regularly.

Prey such as rats, mice, and other small rodents are likely to be active during dawn and dusk, when light is low. These animals can scuttle away into the undergrowth very quickly, thereby disappearing from view and evading capture. Cats need to be stealthy to get near enough for a final powerful dash to grab the prey. The grab must be successful and the prey immobilized quickly or else it will get away – the predator won't get a second chance.

The cat must be able to hunt on its own, not as part of a team like, for example, the wolf or the lion. No backup here or the use of numbers to create an ambush: one animal must get close enough to another (which will be on guard the whole time) and be able to get hold of it and dispatch it on its own.

Perhaps Team Feline looked at the dog as a model to start with, but realized that the cat design must be superior – it must be self-sufficient and it must be stealthy; it must be supple but deadly. Indeed, in order to get to where the prey is the body of this animal must be capable of fairly unique feats of flexibility and power. So Team Feline worked on a design that incorporates a long flexible spine with rounded vertebrae for ease of turning, a tail that can be used for balance, highly mobile joints and ligament and muscle attachments adapted for ease of movement. They kept the clavicle (collar bone) slim and rather than attaching it to the shoulder, as it is in humans, they let it float in muscle, freeing up movement (and making it easy for a cat to carry out tasks such as walking along narrow ledges). They reduced the shoulder blades to allow the cat to swing its shoulder along with its leg, again adding to the length and the fluidity of movement without compromising power. The cat also walks on its toes – the pads are the equivalent of our toes plus the part of the foot in front of the ball. The extra length allows them to get a long stride, touch the ground lightly, and move on again. They made the hind quarters powerful to push the body forward and the front quarters to assist in stopping movement. The body can move from a walk pattern to a run and then to a gallop in which the back legs hit the ground together and push off; the spine bows and lengthens and allows for greater stride length. When it comes to a large leap, the cat can jump five to six times its own length.

All of this would allow the body to get to the prey and pounce on it – but what then? Imagine a small animal running for its life: it is extremely fast and can change direction in an instant – trying to grab with just jaws would be clumsy. Wolves manage it, but then they have the bonus of having several jaws coming at the prey in different directions as the pack closes in. The cat needs to make a successful grab almost immediately. Of course, Team Feline will need to add weapons to the front feet to allow the cat to grab the prey and hang on to it – claws (the sharper the better) would be excellent. However, claws would make silent movement much more difficult and the constant wear and tear from walking on them would blunt them quickly – like the claws of a dog, which help give it grip for the chase, but which are not of much use for anything else. Team Feline were not to be put off – they came up with a brilliant design: a set of razor-sharp weapons that are normally kept sheathed and sharp but can be brought into play the instant they are needed. While the cat is walking or resting, the claws are tucked away in the pads, but when required the muscles and tendons of the foot pull the end bone of the toe forward and this automatically pushes the claw out and straightens it so that it is firm and strong. The nails of the claws are backward facing, so that when they hook into the prey, they prevent it from escaping. Brilliant enough, but a dog with retractable claws would still not be good enough. The cat must be able to use these weapons in a flexible way, not just be straight-legged. Thus, the cat has a flexible "wrist" that allows it to turn its paw for hunting, getting its prey to its mouth, and is additionally useful for grooming, climbing, and so on. Indeed, these built-in crampons are also ideal for climbing and help the cat to follow prey or to escape from danger. When they are tucked away, the cat walks on cushioned pads that give it a light silent step.

So the flexible forelegs and claws can be used to grasp the prey, get it to the mouth, and pass it into a strong jaw with powerful teeth – in particular, long and pointed canine teeth. These are used with extraordinary finesse rather than brute force – they slide between the neck vertebrae and sever the spinal cord very cleanly and quickly, with accurate precision.

The Team should be very satisfied thus far – the body of the cat is lithe, supple, and strong – it can move silently, has a powerful leap, and can catch prey with its retractable claws. It is not designed for long sprints or running prey down, but for stealth and surprise. So far so good. But how to find the prey?

Some sort of radar system built to respond to the appropriate kind of prey would be excellent. What could it home in on? Small animals make rustling noises as they move around in the undergrowth; they also make sonic and ultrasonic squeaks. If these could be picked up, that would give a starting point. Team Feline thought about the ear of the cat – it must be able to hear sounds in the range made by the prey, much of it in the human ultrasonic range. In fact, they gave the cat one of the largest hearing ranges in the animal kingdom (surpassed only by the dolphin and the horse) and spanning 0.5 octaves – a range of frequencies from 30 to 50,000 hertz. So that the cat can hear when there is prey in the field – the area of the field is somewhat large and the prey is somewhat tiny and the cat is not built for running long distances – the Team added a couple of radar dishes, similar to those used to gather information from the stars, right on top of the cat's head. These ears, with large ear flaps called pinnae, are controlled by more than 12 different muscles and can swivel independently through 180 degrees. Internal ridges or corrugations channel and amplify the sound down into the internal ear. By calculating the difference in the time taken to reach each ear, an internal computer can pinpoint the source of the sound very accurately – the cat will be able to distinguish between sounds 3 inches (8 cm) apart at 7 feet (2 m) or 15 inches (40 cm) apart at 70 feet (20 m), accurate enough to get the cat near so that it can see the prey before pouncing.

One of the specifications Team Feline had at the start of the challenge was to ensure that the cat could function in the low light available when its prey is on the move. Thus, another specialist review would be necessary to tackle the problem. For humans, twilight is a very difficult time to see: colors become very muted and definition is lost – brown mice would melt away into the grey undergrowth without too much trouble. We struggle to see human-sized animals in this light.

This will have been one of the team's greatest challenges – the eye would have to fit on to quite a small head and be designed to make the best of low light levels. So the designers made the eye itself quite large in proportion to the head (another feline feature humans find very attractive) and gave it a pupil that can open to about three times the width the human eye can. This lets in as much light as possible on to the retina, the sensitive layer of cells at the back of the eye that conveys signals to the brain. They packed in more rods – the specialized cells that respond to light – at the expense of cones, the cells that are responsible for color sight. Thus, the cat sees much better in low light, but will have sacrificed some ability to see color – it will probably be able to see muted blues and greens, but not reds.

Then they fitted the turbo system. Using the principle of re-routing exhaust gases through the engine in a car to use again, a special reflective layer of cells called the tapetum lumium reflects light that has not been absorbed by the eye first time around and gives the retina a second chance to use it. The reflective layer can be seen when a cat is caught in car headlights or in the flash from a camera and looks silvery green. Team Feline should have patented it – it made someone a fortune when applied to devices placed in the middle of the road to aid night driving! This maximum efficiency gives the cat forty to fifty times better night vision than humans. Not content with this, the designers added some cells that are very sensitive to movement, allowing the cat to pinpoint its prey very quickly.

The only problem with this brilliant system is that its sensitivity may cause problems in the strong light of day – especially for a desert-dwelling animal that is active during the daytime too. Other designs, such as the bush baby, have large and very sensitive eyes, but are purely nocturnal – they do not have to deal with the full glare of the daytime sun. So the designers added a safety feature: the ability to shut down the system when the light is bright. The beautifully colored protective shield that surrounds the light-sensitive pupil can be drawn right across, leaving only a thin slit to let the light through – this is the pupil. A second set of much stronger shutters (the eyelids) can then shut down horizontally for maximum protection. Indeed, Team Feline were so proud of their stunning design that they added a third eyelid that can be drawn across the eye in times of danger to it. This third eyelid is hidden away and seldom seen, occasionally being raised halfway when a cat is not well.

These beautiful precision instruments are positioned at the front of the skull and give the cat a wide field of vision – a combination of the fields used by animals that hunt and those that are hunted (which, of course, can include the cat itself). The cat focuses best at a distance of 7 to 20 feet (2–6 m), the distance from its prey it must reach before it makes that final and all-important strike.

Thus, the cat has good eyesight in the day and well into what we would term darkness. However, when it is truly dark even the cat will have difficulty seeing. If it is following a sound and moving through the undergrowth, how can it avoid the danger of obstacles in the way? Could Team Feline come up with something else innovative? Being exceptionally inventive, they came up with a very simple system that acts like a sensory force field around the cat but is especially concentrated around all that sophisticated equipment on the head! A series of long, firm but flexible hairs protrude around the head and on the elbows, with smaller hairs over the body on the coat. These are exceptionally sensitive to movement. Called vibrissae, or (in the case of those around the mouth) whiskers, they are sensitive to a movement of 5 nanometers – that is, about one two-thousandth of the width of a human hair! Any tiny movement causes bundles of nerves around the base of the hair to send information to the brain or other sensory systems so that the cat can react quickly to avoid obstacles. Indeed, so sensitive are these hairs that they will probably be able to feel eddies of air around obstacles and give the cat a detection system that doesn't even rely on touch.

Another little problem that faced the team was to consider how to get the sharp teeth into position for the nape or killing bite without dropping the prey (which would scamper off immediately and become lost in the undergrowth, resulting in a lost meal). As it gets very close to its prey, a cat will need a different means of being aware of where it is. Step in the whiskers and sensitive hairs again – make the whiskers mobile and they can be held flat on the face or almost straight out in front and used as sense organs. As the cat pounces and grabs the prey and brings it to its mouth, the whiskers are thrown forward and act as another hand to let the cat know what is happening at close quarters. An additional row of sensitive hairs along the upper lip also tells the cat about the position of the prey in its mouth – which way the fur or feathers are lying – and hence where the neck is. This intimate knowledge allows the cat to kill the prey easily.

The team certainly outdid itself with ideas and innovative design in tackling the bodywork and the main sensors. They produced something that was not only functional, but also very beautiful – the Ferrari of the animal world. However, in order to pull it all together and make it work, they needed a central control unit that could receive all of the incoming information from the sensors and send out information on what to do next. The area set aside for this is not overly large – it can't be too heavy because otherwise the cat will be handicapped in its movement. They used the basic mammalian brain as a template but tweaked it to give some bits more space than others. They had a huge volume of sensory input to deal with: information from the eyes, the ears, and the other touch sensors. With all of this information coming in from the outside world they opted to devote more working power to an area called the cerebellum, which processes these complex, continual signals.

In order to hunt successfully the cat must be able to hold its head (and, by implication, its eyes) level and steady to keep the prey in sight as it moves forward, and to be able to calculate accurately how and when to strike. Thus, a very sensitive sense of balance was a must. By now you won't be surprised to hear that the cat not only has a very sensitive sense of balance, but also a quite extraordinary sense of balance. The organ of balance, the vestibular apparatus, is situated in the inner ear. Consisting of three fluid-filled semicircular canals and lined with millions of tiny hairs, the nerve attachments pick up signals from the hairs as the fluid moves in response to movements of the cat's head. This system is common to mammals; however, the cat has taken it to Formula 1 racing precision. A continual monitoring system that responds automatically to changes in position allows the cat to adapt its position continually and thus maintain its sense of balance seemingly without effort.

But that's not all. Team Feline also developed a self-righting system so that if the cat fell from a height, it could automatically turn around in midair and land on its feet. As it falls, an automatic sequence of events is put into action that turns the cat so that its head is horizontal and upright and then brings its body around. The back of the body then swings around too and the cat can land on all fours. Of course, cats do fall awkwardly and if they fall from great heights they will injure themselves. The cat can land unscathed from most tree-height falls, however.

The self-righting sequence is an example of a process that involves automatic responses to signals coming from the vestibular system. Because the cat has to be a successful hunter and thus react very quickly, it has many such automatic responses. You may think that the nervous system works quickly enough via the ordinary system whereby messages come from the outside and into the brain and another is sent out in response. This method uses a little "thinking" time, however, and sometimes this involves too much delay – in a fall, the cat would have hit the deck awkwardly with only milliseconds of delay. Under this automatic system, the information goes directly from the sensor to the muscles and puts into motion a series of pre-programmed movements, making the system lightning fast and giving the cat an edge over both its competitors and its prey.

So Team Feline did a fantastic job. They produced the ultimate predator, the earthbound equivalent of the shark, and one at which we should marvel. It is also adaptable to being affectionate with us, which puts it leaps and bounds ahead of the fish!

Millions of years of evolution have brought the cat to this point, and into the human sphere as well. Team Feline designed a super-animal, the equivalent of a Formula 1 racer. No sensible town car this. If we had wanted Team Feline to design an animal that was purely capable of sitting on our laps and purring, and moving itself to the food bowl a couple of times a day, I doubt it would have ended up looking like a cat. Perhaps we should bear this in mind when we want to change fundamental things about our cats – to make them vegetarian, for example, or to stop them hunting. Our beautiful cats look and act as they do because of their superbly efficient design.

# The Hunter

No study of the cat would be complete without a look at how it hunts – in the context of this book it will give us a better understanding of how all of that amazing feline equipment is put to work and how the animal spends its time when hunting.

The "domestication" of the cat is based on its hunting abilities – it took advantage of a concentration of rodents around stores of grain. The cat is still valued for its hunting abilities in some places, but today, in most cat-owning homes in many different countries, this is probably the least appreciated of the cat's talents. It is the least appreciated in two senses: first, most people do not understand the fantastic design of the cat and its prowess in hunting; second, most owners these days don't actually want their cat to hunt. To be a little more accurate, most don't mind if the cat kills rats or mice (though they would prefer them not to bring their prey indoors, especially if it is not dead), but don't want to see their pet feline killing birds or other small and furry animals. Our expectations for our cats these days are not only that they live alongside us and our other pets, but also that they live peacefully alongside our birds and small mammals.

We have all seen pictures of cats sitting with mice climbing all over them or birds perched on their heads nibbling their ears. While their owners may swear that the cat will not harm its small companion because it has known it since birth, I for one would not want to lay even a small bet on it. It is argued that if the cat grows up with these smaller creatures – potential dinner, after all – it will know they are part of the family group and not harm them. I still wouldn't leave them alone together. Stimulate a cat to follow movement of the right size in the right direction and it will automatically go into a predatory sequence and will have that bite-size morsel in its mouth before even the cat knows it. Millions of years of evolution have created a near-perfect hunter and much of the cat's success lies in the development of automatic or reflex responses that don't even require thinking time. A cat is fast – fast enough to catch a flying bird or a scampering mouse – and, of course, it is clever. I am not the first parent to rush around the local pet shops looking for a certain color of hamster to replace the one that has just been extracted from its snap-together tubing tunnel complex by a shrewd pet cat!

Cats may have to survive through hunting alone if they are not in the vicinity of man and his food, either indirectly via scavenging or by being fed directly. Cats that have been fed may or may not hunt. The control center for hunting is different than that for hunger. Therefore, turning off the hunger control does not necessarily turn off the desire to hunt. No doubt a hungry cat will be a keener hunter, but a full cat may also continue to pursue its prey. Cats will still hunt on a full stomach, perhaps because they usually survive on frequent small meals and so need to keep alert for opportunities. Cats given free access to food will eat between eight and sixteen small meals a day.

## HOW CATS HUNT

Most of us are unaware of the strategies our cats use to hunt – they simply go out through the cat flap and reappear some time later, perhaps carrying a small body of some sort. We may simply find presents on the bed or in the cat's bowl, or come down to the kitchen in the morning and find it awash with feathers.

The cat must be able to hear and identify the sounds of its prey from quite a distance away, to be able to pinpoint the likely position of the prey and then get close enough to it to grab it quickly. From a very young age the cat begins to learn how to interpret all the messages coming to it from its ears, eyes, and other sensory organs. It must learn how to approach different kinds of prey and how to get close enough to be effective in its final pounce. It is not built for pursuit, so stealth and prediction are important.

Cats do employ different hunting strategies, both generally and individually. Some cats move around looking for prey or listening for what they might just come across – this is called the M strategy (M standing for "mobile"). As owners we are probably not aware that cats are even listening as we watch them in the garden. However, we have probably seen our cats undertaking the second approach, the S strategy, where S stands for "sitting and waiting." How often have you looked out and seen the cat sitting and gazing into space seemingly just daydreaming the afternoon away? If you looked more closely you would probably find a small burrow or a tiny pathway or run that is frequently used by one of the garden's little inhabitants. The cat will position itself outside the burrow and sit silently and patiently, staring at a likely spot until something comes out or until the cat itself becomes bored and moves on to a more likely spot. If something does come out, it will wait until it has moved a little distance from the burrow entrance before moving forward and pouncing to prevent it from going back in.

Cats can employ both of these techniques together (they are not bothered by scientists' neat classifications!) depending on the type of prey they are after. Birds on a bird table may require a sit-and-wait strategy; birds feeding off the ground may require a very careful M approach, as birds can see all around them and are constantly checking for danger. The cat must use all of its movement control systems to glide over the ground without attracting attention with sharp or large movements. It may slip in a couple of runs if the bird hops out of sight and then freeze again – similar to the children's game Red Light, Green Light, 1, 2, 3 – stopping still if the subject of its gaze turns around to look in that direction.

Some cats don't bother to hunt birds; others become expert in this 3D hunt. Apparently cats have a natural period of inactivity – a waiting moment – just before they pounce. This is not conducive to bird hunting, because the upwardly mobile prey will often fly away at this point.

When we looked at the cat's senses and its physical attributes and automatic control sequences for hunting, it became clear just how much finesse went into the hunting sequence – down to being able to position the prey precisely enough to slip a canine tooth between the vertebrae at the nape of the neck and sever the spinal cord, causing instant death.

As owners we would probably not dislike the cat doing all this killing so much if we knew that every animal died very quickly and painlessly. Unfortunately, not all cats kill all prey immediately. Some may still be learning their technique and these, probably younger cats, may play with the prey before it dies. Researchers have found that although both sexes of cat will bring home prey, females will do this more frequently than males. This is understandable, because queens will bring home prey for kittens to eat or for them to practice their hunting techniques on once they have reached a certain age. Male cats have nothing to do with kittens so perhaps they are just bringing it into the den for safekeeping.

Why do cats play with prey? Different research has suggested that the act of hunting fills the cat with tension. When it kills, it is still "hyped up" and needs to release this tension, which it does by playing. Researchers who carried out one study of tigers in captivity found that if they made the tigers "hunt" for their food by placing it at the top of a pole and making the big cats climb up and work to get it, the tigers would bring it down, but then leave it for a while before they ate it. The theory is that they had to calm down from the adrenaline rush that accompanied the hunt and catch before they could eat the food.

Female cats with kittens have been found to be much more efficient hunters than females without kittens – no doubt the motivation of four or five hungry mouths to feed, either by producing milk or by bringing home prey, serves to speed up hunts and make more successes of each attempt. Apparently, female cats with kittens are able to hear higher sounds than other cats. Perhaps this is so that they can pick up any distress cries of the kittens, but it may also be because they need to hear the sounds of small animals.

Younger pet cats too are very enthusiastic about hunting. When we eventually let them outdoors, they start to bring in insects and worms, which they have successfully sneaked up on and caught.

They then progress to voles and mice as they become more confident and able to use their skills. From about a year on they will hunt very enthusiastically, and owners of young cats that like to hunt often despair in the first couple of years because of the number of small creatures their pets bring in. However, this enthusiasm does not usually persist at the same level after about three years. Some cats do keep it up, but many become less enthusiastic and prefer to sleep in the sun or watch the birds through the window when it is cold or wet outside.

Cats seem to enjoy hunting and they are certainly highly motivated to partake in this activity. Their natural abilities are honed with practice and patience. We need to make sure that we do not underestimate cats' need to hunt and be aware that we need to amuse the totally indoor cat, which does not have the great outdoors as a playground for this innate activity.

# 6

# Living with Us

The previous chapters have looked at what a cat is and how it lives when it is left to its own devices, how it behaves as it does, and even why it looks like it does. Now we add in another element: people. Indeed, when we look at the domestic cat, it is difficult to cut out the human factor – without us providing centers where food is concentrated and available all year round (artificial situations for a wild cat) the domestic cat may never have come into being. So in a way it is false to look at the natural cat without considering people too. It is useful to see how it behaves and interacts with its own kind, however, and to compare how these behaviors are used in its relationship with mankind.

## WHAT IS IT ABOUT CATS?

Many people have tried to analyze the relationship between cats and humans. Cats are often dismissed as child substitutes. This puts the onus for the relationship on the person rather than on the cat and is somewhat condescending as a result. The attitude probably began at a time when it was not quite so acceptable to be "soppy" about one's animals, and provided an excuse for it for the women involved – and invariably it would be women rather than men who regarded cats so affectionately. Moreover, the cat is regarded by some people as a complete parasite, living alongside us and simply taking everything it can get – food, warmth, and protection – and never doing anything it is told to do or giving anything in return.

Perhaps some of us do treat our cats like children. Indeed, with people delaying having children until later in life and many even deciding not to have children at all, and with the growing number of people choosing to live alone and families not living as close to one another as they once did, perhaps cats are filling a family void and a need to care and nurture. In turn we want something to respond to our nurturing instincts.

For some, the appeal of the cat lies in its physical grace and beauty, while others are attracted by the cat's independent nature. Many people want to live alongside an animal on an equal basis with mutual respect; the cat fits this scenario well. The dog has a pack mentality – for a peaceful life, its position within this family pack must be subordinate to that of the human inhabitants. The dog has to do as it is bidden; it cannot try to take over the house or become aggressive if people step out of line! No such problems with a cat. Respect its choices and it won't run roughshod all over you – and even if it does, it will be wearing velvet slippers!

Perhaps more of a clue to the nature of the relationship between humans and cats lies in the way they behave with us. It is worth reflecting for a moment on the ways their behavior with humans is similar to their interaction with other cats and, perhaps more interestingly, on what features are unique to the cat/person relationship.

## MAKING COMPARISONS

Cats that live closely alongside humans are usually confident with us – they don't raise their hackles in fear and they don't sit in postures that keep the body small and protected, as they would if they felt threatened. They walk confidently to us and often greet us with the "tail-up" response discussed earlier. It is a signal of acceptance and perhaps even a greeting. Kittens greet their mother in this way. The posture also makes the ano-genital area available for investigation and cleaning by the mother. From this perhaps we can conclude that our cats see us as part of their group, something to be confident with and to be welcomed.

Another familiar cat behavior is to rub around us with their heads and bodies; in fact, cat/human rubbing happens more often and with more intensity than cat/cat rubbing. In this way they are picking up some of our scents and also depositing their scent on us – building up a group scent to establish where they belong and who belongs in the group. In groups of feral cats, this behavior is initiated by cats of "lower rank" to cats of "higher rank" – kittens rub their mothers and females rub males. Do they perhaps see us as superior members of their social group? Alternatively, have they learned to use rubbing as an attention-getting signal?

Several aspects of feline behavior point to a maternal type of relationship. Cats retain behavioral patterns with us that are exhibited mainly during kittenhood. Kittens purr almost from birth – they purr as they suck, perhaps to let their mother know everything is fine. The queen will purr as she enters her den – possibly in order to tell her young that they are safe and to encourage them to join in. At present we still don't really know whether it is a communication of contentment or of safety, or a way of encouraging greater interaction. Interestingly, cats will sometimes purr when they are extremely ill or in pain. It is possible that they do so in an effort to try and reassure themselves, or to bring on a more relaxed state of mind, or perhaps as a signal of a need for reassurance. For humans this unique feline sound is very rewarding and is taken as a sign that the cat is happy.

Another kitten behavior humans love is the kneading action that cats undertake on our laps or when they are sitting on a soft woolly blanket. They push their feet forward with a sort of rhythmic action, similar to that of kneading bread, and usually push their claws in and out at the same time. This is truly a kitten behavior as it is executed to stimulate the flow of milk to the nipple while sucking. For a cat, kneading and purring on our laps is similar to a return to that warm and contented position snuggled next to their mother, protected and with a meal imminent or already in the tummy – a position of no responsibility, no fear, and lots of contentment: sheer bliss! So we are probably right to be delighted when our cats behave this way on our laps, although such kneading can be quite painful. This neoteny (a term for baby behaviors carried over into adult life) is a sign that our cats are very relaxed with us, relaxed enough to "return" to a very vulnerable place and time in their lives when they were not able to be the independent creatures they have become as adults.

Cats also let us stroke them, a form of behavior they have to learn to accept. They were groomed by their mother initially out of necessity, as kittens cannot evacuate the bladder or bowel without maternal stimulation when they are first born. They seem to enjoy being groomed around those areas that contain scent glands – the head and face and base of the tail. Is the spreading and mixing of scents encouraged by making the touching of these areas a pleasurable experience?

The most interesting facet of our relationship with our cats is our vocal communication with them. We live in an environment and culture that centers around verbal communication. In groups in the wild, adult cats are rarely vocal with each other. They sometimes revert to high-intensity sounds – yowling, calling, and caterwauling or even spitting and hissing – but rarely make that most feline of sounds, the meow, with each other.

Perhaps it is simply that cats use forms of behavior with us that they usually display only with other cats that do not pose a threat to them. For kittens this would be their mother at those times when they are dependent on her for nourishment and protection. For adult cats it may be other cats with whom they are relaxed – often related cats. Our cats may feel they can also exhibit such behavior in our presence and retain their juvenile characteristics.

A recent theory explaining why two such different species as cats and people can get on so well looked at appeasing pheromones. As described earlier, pheromones are a means of sending a chemical signal that elicits a certain response in another member of the same species. In mammals these chemicals are very complicated and we do not as yet understand them very well. Apparently, female mammals produce a pheromone several days after the birth of their young that makes the baby feel content and gives it a feeling of well-being. The baby too has pheromones on its skin and these, along with the appeasing hormones of the mother, help the formation of that strong mother/baby bond. It is thought that the pheromones produced by people, cats, and dogs are very similar. This may explain part of the attachment or bonding we have with these species. In cats and dogs the production of appeasing pheromones increases after birth and until weaning. After weaning the offspring need to start becoming independent and the drop in appeasing pheromones may help lessen the attachment to the mother. Do these pheromones explain partly why our cats can sometimes seem so relaxed with us?

It is the use of vocal communication that is the most intriguing aspect of our relationship with the cat, however, and which demonstrates a dramatic shift from the animal's usual behavior with other cats. How, and why, has this come about? Has the clever cat found that it can get itself noticed by responding to this very noisy human – a meow to bring attention produces a query as to what the cat wants, or the offer of food? Responding to the human response brings even more attention and this positive reinforcement creates and cements the bond. If cats were able to form human words with those feline vocal cords, I am sure these highly adaptable creatures would be clever enough to work out a way of doing so.

This chapter has been a discussion of the relationship between cats and humans, but in real life the cat living with us is seldom alone. Most of us live in urban or suburban settings with an average of one-and-a-half cats in every cat-owning household. Therefore, if cats live with us, they must also live closely with other cats, something that can be a complicating factor.

# 7

# The Consequences of Living with Humans

We've looked at how the cat lives when left to its own devices. If there is no source of food, then it will probably have a solitary existence living off the land to feed itself and, if female, its offspring. If there is food available, cats may live in groups of females with attendant kittens until the males are old enough to move on. Adult males will have large territories and will move between individual or groups of female cats. In our homes, however, things are not quite so simple.

For cats, the benefits of living with humans are shelter, security, a continuous source of food, warmth, and comfort. However, a cat's owner also assumes he or she can manipulate it. There is a sizable gap between the way we keep cats in our homes and how they choose to live in the wild. Can they swap their natural behavior so easily in exchange for a full food bowl and a warm bed? Of course, the major intervening tool that we have at our disposal in changing our cats' behavior is the facility to change their hormones and thus, to a greater or lesser extent, their behaviors. We can live with them in this way because we almost always make a fundamental change to the motivation of cats – we neuter them.

The main reason we neuter our cats is to control their population. Cats will breed prolifically if left to their own devices, especially if there is ample food around. However, as well as helping to control numbers, neutering brings about a number of behavioral changes that make cats much easier to live with.

Castrating a male cat before it has reached sexual maturity will prevent him from spraying pungent urine in and around the house, cut down considerably on the amount of fighting he will become involved in (and the consequent infections and damage that can result), and reduce his roaming tendencies. Thus, male cats will stay around the home and while they may have spats with other local cats (which are also neutered), there will be little of the caterwauling and out-and-out fighting that accompanies the presence of several intact toms in a small area.

Females too, will be much easier to live with after they have been neutered. An un-neutered female will come into season when the days begin to get longer in the spring and will call for a mate for about a week, repeating this call every two weeks or so if she is not pregnant. She will also try to get out to find a mate. Owners will notice all the local un-neutered toms hanging around, spraying and fighting for the female's attention. If she is not neutered, she will probably become pregnant very quickly and, after nine weeks of gestation, give birth to an average of four kittens. Unless these kittens are neutered, the whole process will begin again when they are around six months old, by which time the mother will have had at least one more litter.

The behavior of an un-neutered female that is not in season is very similar to that of a neutered female. Neutering will only change her behavior during what would have been sexually active times.

Neutering will thus prevent the birth of more and more cats and will remove much unwanted feline sexual behavior of cats. It also allows us to keep more cats together because they will be less reactive to one another.

One way of looking at the differences that neutering makes is to study a group of feral cats that have been neutered. Not a great deal of work has been done on the effect of neutering, but researchers have found that the behavior of males changes slowly. Testosterone will stay in a male cat's system for several weeks after castration and, as it is obviously the prime motivator for many of the cat's behaviors, these too may take a little time to change. Depending on how old it was when castrated, the cat may also have some forms of behavior that it has learned or which have become habits that it may not lose immediately. Researchers found that neutering does curb spraying and aggression, but may not temper roaming to the same degree. Older males which had expanded territories each year still tended to roam quite far – their horizons had already expanded.

Research also revealed that males become more tolerant of members of the group after they are neutered, and also of outsiders. Females tend to interact with males and kittens in their own group, but not a great deal with each other. Studies also found that male kittens do not disperse from the female group in the way they would normally. Are these changes, brought about by neutering, enough to suddenly make the pet cat able to live with other cats in our homes – cats of our choice, cats which are not necessarily related to the original pet?

Neutering our cats irons out a great deal of the differences between male and female behavior, such as the extremes of spraying, excessive fighting and roaming and, of course, of calling, mating, and kitten rearing. However, in general, neutered males will only have slightly larger territories than neutered females: house cats range for about an acre or so around their core territory. Interestingly, research has shown that fighting is equally common in neutered females and males. It also points to neutered males being friendlier to other cats in the household than females – evidence which is borne out by many anecdotal reports from owners.

When we look at the feral group, neutered or un-neutered, there are still gaping differences between the way they choose to live and the way we keep our pet cats. We know that cats will live in groups if there is enough food around and, importantly, enough den areas or resting areas. Female cats seem to keep to themselves or interact with related females, but push new females away. They are more tolerant of having un-neutered male cats around – whether this also applies to neutered males, we are not sure. Studies on the neutered feral group found that male kittens did not disperse the way they normally would – was this because neutered females did not push them away or because they had less motivation to roam? We still have a lot to learn about this area of cat behavior.

Males, on the other hand, tend to fight, spray, and roam less when they are neutered. They are also more relaxed about letting other cats into their areas. Personal experience and that of talking to cat owners and behaviorists seems to point to the suggestion that neutered males are quite happy to become cats within a multi-cat household, are much more laid-back than females, and are more accepting of new cats – not what one would imagine when thinking in broad terms about males and territory. Female cats, however, do seem to resent the introduction of new cats more than males. Their core territory still seems to be very precious and their security depends on it – perhaps because even when they were not having kittens, having a secure, safe place would be vital for them when they eventually did reproduce. Un-neutered males have larger territories that often overlap with those of other males – probably simply because they cannot physically defend such a large area and for the most part want to avoid confrontation until driven to it, which is of course when testosterone comes into play.

Are these things we should be considering when we get our cats? If we want more than one female cat, should we be getting sibling females? When kittens are raised together, they learn to form social bonds with each other through their sensitive period, between about three and seven weeks, that seem to make relationships in later life easier. Should we be more careful about introducing cats into homes where there are already female cats? Should additional cats be male rather than female? How densely can neutered cats live, both in the home and in territories (yards) surrounding their homes? And if they are finding their present living conditions difficult, how would we know? There is so much we just don't know and will have to guess until sufficient research has been done in this area.

Another consequence of living with humans, aside from the possibility of having to share a home with other cats of the human's choice, is that it imposes control on the feline lifestyle. Historically, our relationship with cats has been a very fluid one: they came and went as they pleased. Now we are controlling their times of entry into and exit from our homes, and in some cases not letting them go out at all. How does this affect their welfare?

## WHAT CATS WANT

Trends in keeping cats are changing all over the world. For example, in some areas it is now recommended that cats not be allowed outside. Their claws are removed to ensure they do not damage people or houses. They may indeed be kept safe from outdoor risks, but at what cost to their mental welfare? At the other extreme, cats are still persecuted and cruelly treated in many otherwise very civil countries. Are we worrying too much about a few very well-loved and pampered cats? Perhaps the only thing their owners are guilty of is loving them too much. There are still millions of cats that are starving or suffering from disease or injury, but that doesn't mean we shouldn't look carefully at how we keep our own cats, at how we can use our knowledge for the best, and at what cats want as well as what we want.

In many ways the cat seems to be the perfect pet, but is it too good to be true? In true human fashion, have we found a good thing and then tried to get too much from it? Some people reading this may disagree. They may have a cat that soils in the house, is aggressive to them, or overgrooms itself to the extent of causing itself harm. However, when we consider the available studies in this area, it becomes clear that many of these problems have arisen because we have tried to push the cat too far: impressed by its adaptable nature, we have been led into greater and greater demands from it.

# What Do We Want FROM Our Cats?

So far we have looked at what cats do when left pretty much to their own devices and have briefly touched on some of the obvious consequences of cats living with humans, such as neutering. The question "What do we want from our cats?" obviously has a variety of answers depending on the individuals involved. We may think we live in parallel with our cats and allow them to be independent. However, we do still have quite a few expectations of our cats and these are increasing. Even forty years ago we would have been happy to have one cat that came and went as it desired, having a stroke or cuddle as it – and we – wanted. Many cats still live in this way with their owners, but the advent of cat litter in the 1950s allowed us to control our cats much more – to keep them indoors when we wanted to and to have some control over their lifestyle. Many owners now want a closer relationship with their pets. This may be because the owners live alone and the cat is their sole companion at home, or simply because they are trying to cram a lot into their lives, which inevitably means that everything must be kept under more control.

## WHAT AFFECTS THE INTENSITY OF OUR RELATIONSHIP WITH OUR CATS?

This, of course, is not a simple question and any answer we attempt is bound to be multifaceted. The relationship will depend on the person's desire to interact with the cat; likewise on the part of the cat, as well as on its ability to interact. Before we can look at the relationship as a whole, we need to look at the factors that affect how cats interact with people. These include genetics, early exposure, experience, and the way in which people interact with the cats themselves.

## GENETICS

Like people, the way cats react to the world around them depends on a combination of genetics and experience. Like people too, there are cats that seem to be born bold and confident and others that are always nervous about tackling anything. Researchers who have attempted to characterize cat personalities have found that they can place them in broad categories: cats that are friendly and interact with people; cats that are friendly, but rather reserved; and cats that do not want any contact at all (these were termed "unfriendly"). In a separate study, research revealed that kittens from fathers that were in the friendly category were also friendly. Other researchers found that kittens from friendly fathers were also more likely to go up to novel objects and investigate them – they were more confident and bolder in general, so perhaps this also gave them a confidence with their interactions with people and their willingness to interact was interpreted as friendliness. Researchers who study people have found they can establish whether a baby is bold in nature or not by about the age of nine months, through studying the ways they react in certain circumstances. A nine-month-old baby would be the equivalent of a kitten of about three to four weeks in age – already trying solids and trying to explore around the nest – so the comparison actually fits very well.

We often tend to split our pet cats into pedigrees and mixed breeds. Pedigrees could be defined as cats that come from a pre-defined group – the genes available for them to use come from animals that look similar in many of their physical characteristics – be it coat color or length, or shape of body, size of ears, or color of eyes. Individuals are selected to comply with a set of characteristics that are defined for that breed. However, if we are selecting cats on looks, are we also selecting for certain behavioral characteristics that are within that group already? When we look at some of the breeds, it is obvious that they do have trends of behavior within them. For example, Siamese cats are often very interactive with their owners and demanding of attention and tend to be quite vocal in their interactions. Persians, on the other hand, are less likely to be as active and are much quieter. However, within all cats, be they pedigree or mixed breed, there is a wide range of characteristics and it is said that individual personalities of cats in general, breed or no breed (mixed), span the complete range – you might have a quiet Siamese or a very active Persian. These may be the exceptions within the breed, but individual behaviors still arise that do not comply with the norm. We can guess what is likely to happen in some breeds, but certainly not all – many behave in as wide a range of ways as is possible within the cat kingdom.

# DOES COAT COLOR HAVE AN EFFECT ON BEHAVIOR?

There has been a great deal of research into coat color and temperament and there are many anecdotal stories about certain types and colors, such as tabbies or tortoiseshells. Some researchers have reported that black cats may be more tolerant of high densities of numbers than cats with the agouti gene (this gene produces a wild-type coat that resembles that of a rabbit). Others suggest that cats with the red or tortoiseshell gene are quicker to react if they feel uneasy. Certainly many people report that tortoiseshell females (in fact, tortoiseshells are almost always female) are demonstrably intolerant of handling when they do not want to be touched, and that they react strongly to other cats being introduced into the household. That said, no definitive studies have been done in this area and we cannot make firm conclusions on this point. There are several speculative reasons for linking coat color and behavior – if some of the genes that control coat color are placed close to genes which control behaviors or senses, then certain behavior traits or input of sensory information may accompany certain colors. Moreover, the chemicals available for and used in coat pigmentation may also be associated with brain function and the availability for one may have some effect on the other. Lastly, pigment may directly affect the senses – white cats may be deaf because of a defect in the gene that controls hearing, which is associated with the gene for white coats. This is a topic that will no doubt run and run – are redheads more reactive than blonds? – and we may have all sorts of personal reasons for agreeing or disagreeing. And while the science may not as yet be up to speed on this issue, it continues to be a fascinating subject for speculation and conviction, based on personal experience!

## TIMING OF EXPOSURE TO PEOPLE

There is a period in a young kitten's life when it is very receptive to forming attachments to other animals. Known as the "sensitive period," it lasts from the age of about three to eight weeks. During this time attachments are formed easily and quickly. If kittens experience people and handling during this period, they are likely to be able to form relationships with them in later life and to be friendly pets. If they do not, then it can be difficult for them to become confident pet cats. This is the reason why feral cats seldom make good pets: they can form attachments, but if they have missed this sensitive period, it takes a great deal longer and much more effort to acclimate them to domestic living – in many cases, this will not happen other than from a distance. This highlights the thin line between the pet and the wild or feral cat – one is "domesticated" and the other is not. The question is not simply one of genetics, therefore; early experience is also vital. It is thought that the stimuli that kittens receive during this period act to promote fast growth and development of nerve connections in the areas of the brain that control social behavior and the forming of attachments. This social behavior can be directed at people if they are in the kitten's sphere of exposure at this time. Researchers have found that the more often kittens are handled regularly during the first forty-five days of life (up to a plateau of about one hour a day), the friendlier they will be to humans; indeed, it will affect their attitude to people quite dramatically. They will be much more confident in the way they approach new objects or situations than kittens which have not had this handling.

## MATERNAL INFLUENCE

As discussed above, fathers can contribute genes for confidence that may result in friendly kittens. Of course, mothers too, contribute genetically to their offspring. However, they also have an influence because of their attitude and behavior to people. Father cats have no input into kitten upbringing, so they can have no influence in this way. Kittens learn a great deal by observation, and a friendly mother that is happy to have her kittens handled and will let them interact with humans, will encourage the kittens themselves to behave in a friendly manner toward humans. By the same token, a nervous mother reacting with fear to humans will convey danger to her kittens.

## EXPERIENCES OF PEOPLE

Even though the sensitive period is a time when experience of people will bring about a dramatic difference in a cat's attitude to people, subsequent experiences will also have a great effect. Cats learn quickly and if they have been frightened or hurt, they will take avoiding action to ensure their safety is not threatened in a similar way. Thus, they will take avoiding action at the first sign of danger. This may simply be the appearance of a person, or even certain ages or sexes of people. Many cats have a fear of men, probably because they tend to talk and act rather more loudly than women – they are often less predictable in their behavior, from a cat's point of view, and can appear to be more threatening.

## HOW PEOPLE APPROACH CATS

Women have traditionally been more involved with the care of cats than men. One very interesting study examined the way cats and people who were not familiar with each other reacted together. The researchers looked at a sample of men, women, boys, and girls. When they let the cats initiate the investigation of the people, they found that the cats approached everyone in a similar way and a similar number of times. However, when the people were allowed to interact with them, differences became apparent. In general, the men interacted with the cats from a sitting position and the women, boys, and girls got down to the cat's level. The children tended to approach the cats, whereas the adults waited for the cats to approach them. The boys tended to approach the cats more often than the girls and even followed withdrawing cats (which the researchers felt the cats did not like). The women interacted with the cats from further away and talked to them as they were approached; they also stroked them more when they came close enough. The cats reacted to the encouragement and were happy to interact and to comply with such treatment.

Another study showed that if a person responds to a cat when it wants to interact with them, then the cat in turn will comply with the person who wants to make contact – the more the owner does, the more the cat responds, and vice versa; it is a mutually responsive and positive relationship. Presumably, the initial requirement is a cat that is happy to interact – one researchers would put in the "friendly" box in the first place.

# BRIBERY

We can use certain things cats like to cement their relationships with us. Food can be a motivator for interaction, as can attention. The warmth of a fire or a cozy room can be used to coax a shy cat to share space with people, or even to get onto a lap. Different cats are motivated by different things – prawns may be irresistible to one cat, whereas another will not be in the least interested in doing anything for food. This can be one of the major difficulties in training cats – finding something that they find more rewarding than doing what they want to do!

## COMPETITION

If only one cat and one person live together, then the opportunities for a one-to-one relationship are high, if both are willing. It may seem obvious, but researchers report that the smaller the family, the more attention the cat gives to each person. Single cats spend more time interacting with owners than cats in homes with lots of other felines. Interestingly, owners of single cats were less bothered about the cat being fussy and more tolerant of its curiosity than owners of lots of cats. However, this is hardly surprising – parents with a single child may be much more tolerant of demanding attention, making a mess, or misbehaving. Multiply this up several times (and more) with more children and the situation can become intolerable, no matter how much you love them. Not only will more cats interact with owners in total, but they will also interact with each other. Often this will not be friendly interaction (just like children!) and there will be situations to try and sort out. In this way, caring for more cats becomes harder work, and owners may feel guilty that they haven't been fair to all the cats, or that not every cat has gotten the attention it deserves or needs.

These are some of the factors that influence how and why cats react with people and they suggest something about the extent to which they might approach interaction. But this chapter is about what people want from their cats.

People live with cats in a wide range of situations, from feeding feral cats on the farm or in the yard to keeping a single cat totally indoors in a very close relationship. We can manipulate the intensity and closeness of the relationship to some extent by first of all choosing which cats we interact with and then how we actually keep them.

Many people find great satisfaction in taking the wildest version of our domesticated cat, the feral, and becoming responsible for its care at arm's length. The cat will usually have been neutered, but aside from this handling (which usually requires a cat trap to catch the cat and careful handling at the veterinarian's office to ensure nobody is injured until the cat is anesthetized), it is then allowed to go back to its site and its health is monitored from a distance by its feeders. Recatching ferals is very difficult – they learn what a trap is after being caught once and are unlikely to enter it again. Thus, they have to stay fairly healthy on their own, but their food is provided by carers. Some of these cats can become quite friendly – they will certainly sit and wait until their feeders come and will greet them as they bring the food. Some may tolerate a stroke or pat, but many will simply stay at flight distance – the distance at which they can safely dash away should danger arise. While this may not make for a close relationship, it is a nurturing one and can be very satisfying for both sides.

The opposite end of the spectrum is the totally indoor cat, which centers its life and waking hours around the presence of its owner. Many such cats are pedigree and some are breeds that form strong bonds with their owners anyway, such as Burmese or Siamese. These breeds are more interactive than some others and can be almost dog-like in their devotion. They are also very bright animals which need to be kept interested and prevented from becoming bored. Thus, their interest and their activity have no external component and can become very focused upon their owners; the interactions can be very close. This is the kind of relationship that some cat owners want too, but it puts a great deal more responsibility on them in terms of keeping the cat amused and not frustrated, especially when owners are at work or even when they just go out. Such cats can become overattached or bored – see chapter 10 for more on this subject.

Of course, most cat owners fall between these two extremes: they have one or two pet cats that may have access to outside some or all of the time, and the cats fit their lives in around that of the family or person in a way that is mutually convenient to both. When we look at what we want from our cats, it is necessary to cover all these relationship choices as well as the conventional one, because it is in the extremes that we see the cat pushed to its limits.

## DO WE WANT INDEPENDENT CATS?

One of the most obvious benefits of owning a cat as a pet rather than a dog is that it is much less onerous in terms of being responsible for its behavior and its activities, both within the home and out with the public at large. Cats' popularity as pets has grown for both of these reasons. On the whole, cats are very happy to live with us, but retain their independence as well.

Most cats that go outdoors happily live a Jekyll-and-Hyde type of existence, becoming kitten-like indoors and enjoying us feeding them and touching them; they relax and lap up the attention. Outdoors they patrol like tigers, hunt a little if they feel like it, and have the odd set-to with the cat next door if it happens to be around.

Their adrenaline-rush requirement satisfied for the day, they then return inside to become couch potatoes again. For most owners, this is absolutely fine – the cat comes and goes as it wishes. Some people close the cat flap at night to try and protect the cat from cars and creatures of the night, and to protect small mammals from the cat at dawn and dusk. Most cats are still free to do as they wish in the day, indoors or out.

Other people neither expect nor want independence from their cat. As usual, we need some science to try and find out what different people want from their cats – one such survey found that owners of cats that had a very free type of lifestyle and came and went as they wished, rated their cat's independence highly and felt that this is how cats should be. Conversely, owners of cats which did not go outdoors at all didn't value independence highly in their pets, but wanted them to stay in and be close to them. Presumably, those who rated independence highly would rather not have a cat than keep one indoors all the time because of the risk posed by a busy road nearby or a dangerous neighborhood.

## CLEANLINESS

Part of the reason for the phenomenal success of cats as pets is their cleanliness. Their toilet habits can be left to occur naturally in the great outdoors (usually in the neighbor's finely tilled vegetable garden!), or can be controlled and managed by the use of a litter tray. And unless you count irate neighboring gardeners, most cats' toilet habits do not cause social problems in the way that toileting in the street has for dogs.

Cats are also physically clean. In general, short-haired cats seldom bring mud or dirt into our homes. Long-haired cats with access outdoors do tend to lend themselves to carrying in bits of sticks and leaves (and even the odd slug) to our houses. Our semi-long-haired cat named Smokie has been rechristened Debris because of the ring of bits and pieces that are left on the cushion or bed after he has had a grooming session. Mud, which seems to fall off the delicate paws of the short-haired cat, hangs on as Debris moves through the house and finally decides to snuggle down on the newly changed cream comforter or in the ironing basket recently filled with clean shirts for the week ahead. However, in general cats are clean in all their habits and do not make our homes grubby in the same way dogs do. They certainly don't smell (not to the human nose, anyway) and don't slobber, so our homes don't have that "*eau de* damp dog" that is so endearing of their canine cousins. People with impeccable homes are thus generally happy to have cats around – we expect our cats to be clean and to use a tray if provided, and most cats happily comply.

## NONDESTRUCTIVE

When we talk about destructive behavior in pets, we immediately think about dogs, which often tend to chew up their owners' homes if they are left alone. We have all heard of separation anxiety and how dogs, because they are of necessity pack animals, become distressed if they are separated from their pack. They have to learn how to cope with being alone and owners have to help them to do this if they want to have normal lives (such as being able to come and go without the dog eating the carpet or couch in their absence). We don't really think of our cats as destructive although they can cause damage with their scratching habits. Some cats don't scratch furniture, carpets, or walls at all in their human homes. Others have a favorite armchair or carpeted stairs that they just cannot resist

76

ripping to shreds! Cats can be destructive, but the difference is that most cat owners seem to have a different attitude about cats doing this than do the owners of dogs.

When Fido chews up the new bean bag, it is seen as a deliberately destructive action (even though it may be in response to the emotional stress of isolation). In cats, such an act is not seen as a premeditated action or destruction for the sake of it; it is seen as a claw-sharpening act carried out in the wrong place. Owners often try and introduce a scratch-post, with which they attempt to coax the cat into redirecting the behavior on to an acceptable area. They accept that it is a natural behavior in their cat. Having said that, sometimes the front claws of cats are routinely removed to prevent destruction in homes – perhaps a sign of a fundamental difference in the attitude toward cats (or furniture) between the two sides of the Atlantic. In the UK, for example, de-clawing is frowned upon. People there have more outdoor cats and worry that by removing claws their pets will not be able to climb or to get themselves out of trouble or will come off worst in a cat fight because they cannot defend themselves. In fact, the Royal College of Veterinary Surgeons considers the operation unnecessary.

Cats scratch for a variety of reasons. One is claw sharpening; another is to mark an area, both physically and via scent deposition from glands on the bottom of the feet. And like the anxious dog that may chew objects, a cat may also be motivated to mark more if it feels the need – perhaps because it does not feel secure, because it feels threatened by other cats, or because of changes to its environment.

Differences between attitudes and lifestyles are very common, no matter where people live. One such minor difference seems to be expressed in the way people decorate their homes. Trend-setters say that using wallpaper to decorate homes is very popular. This observation brings to mind conversations that I had with cat owners at a series of pet roadshows. On answering questions from pet owners I inevitably receive a lot of queries about behaviors – why the cat behaves as it does, how to understand what is happening and, if the behavior is a problem, how to try and solve it. During these roadshows, it became very evident from a number of questions on this subject that scratching off wallpaper was high among feline behavioral problems. People simply did not expect their cat to be so destructive in the house. This query had not been evident at other roadshows elsewhere in the country, and on inquiry we found not only that wallpaper was commonly used to decorate homes in this particular area, but also that it often had raised contours or the effect of expensive fabric. These more elaborate – and of course more expensive – wallpapers were the cats' favorites!

On further inquiry it appeared that the cats often scratched wallpaper in the vicinity of the front door or entrance into a room (which makes sense in marking terms). It also became apparent that the cats played with the flakes of paper that were shredded off. Do cats enjoy the sensation of pulling their claws through wood or carpets? Is the motivation to sharpen them rewarded by a feeling of enjoyment? Does embossed wallpaper provide a little too much pleasure? I have a feeling that the cats' initial marking and claw-sharpening experiments on the walls resulted in quite a lot of fun – not only in the sense of dragging claws through the paper and marking it, but in pulling off the bits of paper afterward and playing with them. Suggestions that owners might use paint instead of wallpaper found little favor, and I suspect those cats are still enjoying the thrills of wallpaper removal while their owners grit their teeth at the wanton destruction!

## COMPANIONSHIP

Cats do make excellent companions and are often very sensitive to our moods and needs. They provide a very personal companionship. People who own dogs often make new acquaintances, or at least nodding acquaintances, through walking their pets – people will be far more ready to have a chat or interact first by asking about the dog, and then chatting more generally once there is a focus and an ice-breaker for the conversation. Aside from the very friendly cat that sits on the wall and enjoys a stroke from every passerby, it will not be evident to strangers whether people own cats or not. The cat/human relationship is very one-to-one and interaction with others will not be a motivation for getting a cat.

Researchers examined the way in which we perceive the response and support we get from our cats and have found that we do not regard them as replacing humans in our need for social interaction, but as a genuine source of support, especially when attachment to the cat is strong. Our cats can provide this strong help when we need them and are very important to us. Research has also revealed that cats can help to improve the mood of depressed owners.

## TO BE LOVED

We want our cats to like us. We don't expect them to heel like dogs or to be obedient; we don't expect them to rescue us in a fire, or attack the burglar trying to get away with our savings. In fact, we don't want many of the characteristics attributed to their canine cousins, including protection; having a cat will never make you feel safe. However, we do want to be recognized, to be greeted, and perhaps treated a little differently than the way a stranger would be. Cats can do this, even in circumstances where it would seem that they are not really attached to anyone – feeders of feral cats will be delighted that the cats they feed recognize them as they come, do not run from them, and may even allow themselves to be touched on occasion. This is akin to the enjoyment we get from interacting with some of our wild native animals – feeding or watching badgers or wild birds, for example.

For others, the relationship with a cat must be very intense: they do love their cats fiercely and they do want some sort of feedback. We have to remember that the cat is not a pack animal. The dog is an obligate pack animal – it wants and needs to be part of a group and has developed ways of keeping the group together, through problems generated both externally and internally to the pack through threats and misunderstandings. Because of this, the dog will count man and his family as the pack and so will protect it accordingly – many of our breeds, such as Dobermans or Rottweilers, have been bred to have a more fully developed protecting instinct than others.

A survey of owners found that indoor cats were rated more highly as more active and interactive with their owners. The cats often initiated the interaction. Outdoor cats were rated as less curious than indoor cats. Did outdoor cats seem less curious because they were not always on hand to interact with their owners, because they used up their energies outdoors, and perhaps slept more indoors? Indoor-only cats have less outlets for curiosity, for expending energy – both mental and physical – and are more likely to look to their owners for stimulation. Thus, while the contents of a handbag may not seem very exciting to a cat that has just chased off a couple of local felines, stalked and caught a mouse, and climbed a tree for the fun of it, they may represent something extremely exciting for the indoor cat, without such external adventures in its life.

Interestingly, outdoor cats seem to rub against their owners more than indoor cats, especially when they come in from outside. Are they greeting or exchanging and checking scents to ensure that, scent-wise, their den and refuge has just the right balance of scents to ensure they can relax with the other members who share it?

Other research into this bond between cats and humans has revealed that people rate their own affection for their cat as high if they feel that the cat likes them too. The level of affection was also affected by the cleanliness of the cat, its curiosity and playfulness, and its predictability. This is understandable – if a cat is soiling in the house, it can be very distressing for owners and, much as they like the cat, the feeling of frustration and annoyance may somewhat temper the owners' ability to say that, right at that moment, they love their cat! If it is playful and curious, and if this manifests itself partly in interaction with owners, then the owners' enjoyment of the cat will increase, as will the quoted affection factor. Perhaps predictability was a measure of the closeness of the relationship – how much owners understood their cats and what they were trying to communicate, the need for a cuddle or to be fed, for example. If owners respond to their cats, then cats will respond in kind. This self-reinforcing, rewarding circle makes for a mutually enjoyable relationship – owners love their cats and their cats certainly seem to love them back.

## PLAYFUL

Cats are expected to be playful – the first thing we do with kittens when we get them is to start dangling bits of string in front of them, or give them wind-up toys or Ping-Pong balls to chase. The sight of cats playing is a joy – their grace and athletic prowess, and the daft scrapes they get themselves into when they are overexcited, are a great source of amusement and fascination. Owners of cats that don't play can become worried about their pets for this very reason.

Play is thought to prepare cats for hunting: it helps them to assess their senses and their physical abilities and test them out to see what is possible. It also gives them a chance to interact with each other and learn what is acceptable and what is not.

Some cats take play one step further than the others – they almost cross over into the canine camp of behavior. These cats usually belong to one or two breeds – the Siamese and Burmese. It is not so often seen in the common house cat and is usually confined to these very interactive breeds. Some of these cats actively retrieve – they bring back objects that have been thrown and even put them in front of their owners to be thrown again. Just how this has come about, we are not sure – it may be an extension of a natural behavior of cats bringing back prey to the safety of the den. If these cats then get a reaction from their owners who take the object and throw it, the cat can retain and demand their attention for long periods of time. Both owners and cats enjoy the interaction and so the behavior continues and is used when attention, or exercise, or interaction is required.

## FRIENDLY

The cat is not an exhibitionist pet – cat owners don't seek to frighten people with them or to parade them up a crowded street to get a reaction. Whereas we may meet and interact with lots of strangers with dogs, only friends or close associates are invited into our homes for long enough to find out about our cats. It still takes a little time for the cats to approach them and to make friends – if the friend can pat the cat and even elicit a purr we are delighted. It can be very disappointing to own a cat that runs and hides as soon as anyone comes into the house – sharing our cats is a somewhat intimate affair, but one that owners like to carry out with selected friends and relatives.

## TO FIT IN WITH OUR LIVES

Cats live for about fourteen years on average, and often into their late teens or even their twenties. We may get our first cat while we are single. We may be out working all day, but enjoy sharing the companionship they give us in the evening and on weekends when we are relaxing. The cat learns to center its life around ours, waking when we are around and sleeping when we are out. The house is pretty quiet most of the time and the cat gets to know selected friends who may visit on the weekend or evenings.

Almost inevitably one of these friendships blossoms; a couple weds and adjustments have to be made. The cat may have to find an alternative nighttime spot because it no longer has half the bed available to it, or because the new person does not appreciate having his or her toes pounced on midway through the night. Cuddling up on the sofa requires a bit more determination to get to the lap the cat wants – or may become easier, because there are now two laps available. On the whole it does not change life too much and there are certain benefits.

If a third person suddenly joins the family – a small, helpless bundle that smells strange and is often very noisy – the situation becomes more demanding. Suddenly the whole routine of the house is changed; the cat is not allowed in all of the rooms and is moved out of some very swiftly. There seems to be activity at strange times of the day and night. Again, there are benefits: mom and baby are around a great deal and the cat may even be able to get an extra cuddle while the mother sits and feeds for hours when the baby is very new. For most cats, this is not a problem and they soon adapt. For some very people-orientated cats, however, it can be distressing, simply because they cannot have their owners on tap as they had previously. The cat is not now the center of attention and this, with the disturbing new smells and sounds, can make the cat very unsettled. With these cats it is best to prepare them somewhat for the imminent arrival of the baby and the changes which will occur – owners need to distance themselves a little and limit access before the birth so that the cat does not find such a gulf of difference when the baby arrives

A growing family often leads to a move to a new house. When this happens, the cat has to readjust to the new territory and come to grips with the gangs of other cats or dogs outside that must be negotiated when going out for a stroll.

Babies turn into toddlers (often rather dangerous for cats), and more babies come along and less time is available for the cat. The cat learns to avoid small grasping hands and keep its tail up and out of the way when it sits on the windowsill or other high spots, which it now values greatly.

During this time, it is quite likely too that owners will either positively choose to get another cat, or even a dog, or that a cat will turn up from somewhere (uninvited) and need a good home. Move over a bit more, original cat! Keep that puppy under control and learn to ask for more food, because it finished off the breakfast you only ate half of this morning, which you meant to return to later! Find somewhere higher to rest and feel safe. In fact, a dog does not really spell serious trouble. Another cat coming in causes much more upset and a large adjustment is required in almost everything the original cat has taken for granted, such as the security of the core part of the home, the ability to wander around the house without cause for concern, and having to cope with strange feline smells. The house, which once was quiet and calm, is always active from the presence of a person or a pet and the cat has to adapt its lifestyle accordingly.

Growing children bringing their friends home mean more changes – some good, some bad – and the cat learns how to avoid the ones it doesn't like and enjoy the others. The same rule applies to other pets and cats in the neighborhood.

Some cats will even live long enough to see the children leave home and peace return! Many will experience a change in the make-up of the mix of the adults in charge and with the change come more or less children, other pets, and perhaps another change of home. Still the cat adapts.

These are lifetime adaptations, but there are also daily adaptations to our human rhythms – rather different to the feline rhythm. Although cats will hunt during the day and at night, the time when they are most active is dawn and dusk, when the small creatures they hunt will be active. When cats live with us, they adapt their time of sleeping and activity to suit us. While some of us do have cats that try to wake us as the dawn is breaking, most cats will learn to wait until owners are up and about before making their presence known.

# TO HUNT OR NOT TO HUNT

There are now few situations in which pet cats are required to hunt to pay for their shelter and a little bit of extra food, although some farm cats will still be kept in this manner. And while there may be added (and usually unseen) benefits of cats keeping rodents at bay around the home, most owners would prefer that their cats didn't hunt at all. Most people are now quite far removed from seeing blood in tooth and claw. The beautifully prepared meat we buy at the supermarket, which has already been skinned or boned, means that the nearest we have to get to basic food is a quick division to bite-size pieces with a sharp Sebattier knife – quick and clean and no mess. We are not used to seeing suffering or death and don't enjoy the presents from our cats that we find on the kitchen floor in the morning. There is considerable pressure from conservationists to prevent cats from killing a small mammal and bird population, which is already suffering from changes in farming practice that have removed a great deal of natural habitat.

# NO SEXUAL BEHAVIOR

Apparently people don't have a preference for the sex of the cat they keep – they are just as happy with males or females. This is probably because most of us have neutered cats and both males and females that have been neutered behave in much the same fashion toward us – and, of course, don't display any sexual behavior. Neutering has a very leveling effect on behavior and irons out many gender differences. If we had to live with intact animals – males spraying, roaming, and fighting, and being probably more aggressive with us when we stroke them, or with females calling and having lots of kittens we have to re-home – we would probably have a preference,

or simply not be so fond of cats as pets. For stress-free living in a high density of cats that behave in a predictable way (one of the values rated highly by owners as a factor in their affection for their cats), neutering is a necessity.

## FITTING IN WITH OUR BELIEFS

After reading chapter 5, it will become very evident that the look and behavior of the cat stems from its requirements to be an excellent hunter. The cat's very physiology relies on meat to stay healthy – it is about the most meat-centered animal you will find. Humans, on the other hand, are omnivores – we can survive with or without meat and can enjoy manipulating and changing our food as part of our relaxation, hobbies, or culture. We also have the ability to consider the welfare of other animals and decide whether we actually want to eat them or not. Our physiology makes the choice possible.

However, we need to keep these personal beliefs and preferences in check – just because we can survive happily without meat doesn't mean that our cats want to take on this life philosophy. Not only do they not want the choice, they are obligate carnivores and cannot survive without meat. Why, then, do some owners insist on making their cats become vegetarian? They find a food that is plant-based and add the specific nutrients which cats need (most of which must come from the meat anyway).

Nutritionists have worked out what cats need in terms of the major nutrients, so it is possible to put together a diet which is supplemented with these. However, we know much less about all the micronutrients and the interaction of different vitamins and minerals, as well as amino acids and fats that keep cats in peak condition. And think about how the cat is taking to this new diet. Its body has very specific requirements and its senses have been developed to help it acquire them: its sense of smell tells it about the fats and amino acids in food; the tastes which give pleasure will no doubt come from meat-based compounds. The only vegetation cats usually eat is that which can be found in the stomachs of their prey or the bits and pieces of grass they consume, usually when they are feeling unwell or in need of a purge. How do they cope with this vegetable-based diet – do they enjoy it? Is it doing them good? It is almost like taking a Formula 1 car and trying to get it to run on inferior gasoline and then wondering why it is not performing to its maximum.

I am afraid that vegetarian cats are one of my greatest pet peeves – well, not the cats themselves, but the owners who do not realize that their feline Ferrari is not a lawn mower and it needs quality fuel. My advice to those who wish to have a vegetarian cat is to get a rabbit. An animal which has evolved to eat vegetation will certainly not look like or behave like the cat we know and love. So get a rabbit! Many are now kept inside – indeed, house rabbits are supposed to be our fastest growing pet.

## INDIVIDUALITY

The whole concept of cloning animals has made us think about what we would get if we could clone our pet – from all accounts it would not necessarily look like its parent (coat color is not all controlled by genes and, as we have seen already, character is influenced by many things as well as genetics – thus, it may not behave in the same way either). But do we want one cat which is exactly the same as the one before? Most of us enjoy our cats for their individuality, the things they do, or the way they do them that are unique to that cat and if recounted would allow us to identify that cat over others in the household, or even generally. We want our cats to be individuals.

If you have read the earlier chapters of this book, you will also realize that character is a lot more than the product of genes – early experience and the cat's environment can shape it dramatically. Thus, character cannot be guaranteed either – owners wanting an exact replica of their favorite cat may be disappointed. Indeed, while most of us may have had an older cat which was most loved and we never wanted to lose it, it would be very unfair to get another and expect it to be the same – comparison would inevitably be made on just about everything it did. Better to acknowledge that cat as unique and special, and move on to a new and different one, appreciating it for its own personality and individuality.

Scientists have tried to define individuality and to measure it – this is actually very complicated because if you are using different people to record characteristics, then the results could be influenced by the person, too – for example, judging how cats were rated for friendliness or confidence could well be influenced not only by the personality of the judges present, but on their experience of cats and their attitudes. You can make the research more objective and look at how long it might take a cat to investigate something new in the room and record this as a score of confidence or boldness. Of course, it is very difficult to define the subtleties of behavior, let alone to try and find a way of measuring them that is reproducible – sometimes we can only look at very simple things and try to draw conclusions.

How do individual characters come about? Most people understand that the main influences on an individual's character are genetics and experience; experience gained from interacting with the world around us – the cat's environment and the people and animals within it (see the earlier part of the chapter, which looks at what affects our relationship with our cats).

Looking at the characteristics of young cats, what do we find that persists into adulthood? If we choose a kitten for its confidence and friendliness, will this change as it grows? Again, we have no definitive answers. Some people have found that kittens that are inquisitive and active at four months can still be categorized as such at one year old – perhaps, again, linked to this boldness or confidence. They suggest friendliness may change and that how predatory the cat is may also alter. The way in which you define how a cat behaves – for example, whether it is quiet and withdrawn or outgoing – may also depend on the situation in which it is being measured. A cat that is very easygoing in one situation may react very aggressively in a different situation. This sometimes happens when a new cat comes into the house – the resident cat may become jumpy or quick to react aggressively, even to its owners, and may not seem so affectionate. Perhaps this is because it is not feeling relaxed enough to go into kitten mode with owners because of the "intruder" in the house.

# BEAUTY

Most of us choose our cats because we like the color or the pattern of their coat. It would not surprise readers to find that this too has been studied and the results show that our choice is often based on a cat we had as a child, or one we or a friend had owned previously – beauty is indeed in the eye of the beholder. However, when it comes to cats, it is pretty hard to choose an ugly one. There are some rather battered old toms around, as well as those cats that have had a difficult start in life and bear the scars of their traumas, but in general, most cats are very attractive. Thankfully, we are all different and many owners of pedigree cats with special coat characteristics often also keep mixed breeds, enjoying the good old black-and-white mix as much as the pedigrees with the spotted or striped coats.

## WHAT WE DON'T WANT

As an owner of both dogs and cats I feel reasonably qualified to compare the different way people keep their pets. One of the major differences is that very few cat owners want their felines as status symbols – they cannot really be shown off, except to friends in the home, and they certainly aren't used to threaten or frighten people in the macho way some owners display their dogs. Many dog owners tend to be interested in their own breed (probably more than half of these are pedigree) and not in canine kind in general. In my experience, cat owners like cats, be they pedigree or not, the same breed or different. Just about 10 years ago "spangled cats" (cats with a beautifully patterned coat) were bred and sold almost as a fashion accessory – the price was high because they were supposed to be rare and beautiful. There are people who always want something different and will breed a wild species of cat to a domestic cat to try and recreate some of the fabulous wild coat patterns in our pets – the Bengal is an example of this. Others will take a mutation such as hairlessness, which arises occasionally in a kitten, and make it into a breed – the Sphynx, for instance – or we push our breeds to the limit with flat faces or pointed noses. There will always be a demand for something different, but within the cat-owning public, the numbers of such fantasy felines are tiny and most people remain happy with the beauty of their mixed breed or what is available already in pedigree cats. We must hope that the breeders consider the welfare of the cat rather than the novelty value when they manipulate this animal, which most of us feel is beautiful anyway, whatever its type. Some breed clubs are very forward thinking and have tried to ensure that extremes and differences are not valued more highly than health and functionality – always difficult when there is competition for looks.

On the face of it, most of us would say that we have few expectations of our cats. However, looking more closely at the relationship, it seems that perhaps we do. Can these wants be merged successfully with what we want for our cats, and what they want from us?

# What Do We Want FOR Our Cats?

"Happiness" is something most of us would say we want for our cats, but we have no idea how to measure it. We could say that we know when they are content – they seem to be relaxed, are eating well, are physically at the right weight. They seem healthy and not in any pain, are confident in our home and interact confidently with those around them. However, what makes one cat happy may be torture for another. Not all cats are confident animals. Depending on their genes and their start in life, they may be very nervous animals and meeting someone new may be a terrifying, rather than an enjoyable, experience for them. As owners, there are things we can gauge – whether the cat looks happy and does not seem fearful, or whether it chooses to do certain things with us. However, sometimes we take our own needs and expectations as those of the cat – what we want for it may not be what it wants for itself.

## COMPANY?

We humans are group-living animals – we enjoy social interaction and, depending on what motivates us individually, want to work with others, help each other, live within a family, socialize, and generally be with people for a greater or lesser part of the day. Although we may want peace and solitude occasionally, too much can be isolating. It takes a certain special person to be a hermit, and solitary confinement is regarded socially as a serious punishment. We know how lonely we can feel if we are at home alone all day – at such times even a conversation with the window cleaner can become a very important way of making contact with others!

It is understandable, therefore, that when we leave our cats at home while we work all day, we feel that they may be lonely. We don't want them to feel isolated or low and in need of company. This feeling can be reinforced by our cats on our return – they sit and wait for us to turn up, making us believe they have been expecting us for hours and have maintained a vigil in the window, watching every car as it passes by. They then rub around our legs and meow forlornly, running back and forth as we come in. Of course, we love them to miss us and lap up the welcome.

In reality, the cat has probably found a nice warm spot on a radiator or on a sunny windowsill and snoozed happily throughout the day, moving occasionally to follow the sun, have a snack from the ever-full food bowl, or relieve itself in the tray or outside. It may even have made a patrol of the yard or gone on a little hunting expedition before it feels the need for another rest. Around the time you are due home from work, the cat will stir itself and sit in the window to watch your return. Owners who don't leave dry food on tap for the cat will find their return exceptionally well cheered and will be accompanied into the kitchen with much noise and rubbing until dinner is served.

Remember, the cat's ancestor – the African wildcat – is a solitary living species, seldom meeting its own kind except for mating or raising kittens. Our own domestic cat can be solitary or sociable; however, it isn't an obligate pack animal like the dog, or even humans. And while some females may raise kittens together, there are no other aspects of feline behavior in which labor is shared, or there is cooperation – it is every cat for him- or herself.

Most cats will alter their periods of activity to fit in with their owners. This is especially true of cats that are not let outdoors – they can't do the equivalent of stopping in next door for a cup of coffee or going out for some amusement, such as chasing after the ginger tom around the corner. They are very reliant on their owners for activity and stimulation – very little happens unless owners are around.

For these cats, company may be a very good idea – however, it is harder to introduce a new cat to a resident cat where its territory is confined to a small indoor area and there is little room for escape from one another. The way introductions are made in this situation can be very important (see chapter 12). Thus, if you intend to keep cats indoors, it would be wise to think ahead and get two kittens together – siblings usually get on better because they have spent that sensitive socialization period together, a time when bonds can be formed easily.

There are some cats, usually of the more emotional, more reactive, and interactive breeds such as the Siamese or Burmese, who do become very attached to their owners and can suffer when left alone. These may benefit from company – even from a dog, or perhaps from some behavior therapy to help them "get a life" away from their owners. While some owners may enjoy this level of dependence and encourage it initially, it can become very wearing, and going out becomes an extremely guilt-ridden procedure. Most owners will want their cat to retain its independent nature and some sense of feline dignity.

Perhaps the message here is to "know your cat" – don't assume it wants another feline around just because you do, or because you want to assuage your guilt at having to leave it alone for long periods of the day. Some cats are perfectly happy like this and would be very upset at the introduction of "a friend." Others will need someone or something to interact with, depending on their nature and what they may have been used to. However, again, don't assume that, just because two cats got along previously, the same will happen again if you replace one that has been lost – it is never that easy! I would not dream of suggesting that a lonely person needs just anyone to come and live in the home for company. Close-quarter living needs characters that like, or at least can tolerate, each other. The same is true of our cats. We are already aware that each cat has a very individual personality. It would be arrogant to think that we can force several together and expect them to become bosom buddies.

Sometimes we use the excuse of the cat needing company because we want to get another cat. There is nothing wrong with wanting more felines in the house – cats are eminently desirable. However, acknowledging this motivation can make our approach a little more measured and make us less expectant that the resident cat should be grateful! The onus is back on us to try and make it work.

## DO WE WANT OUR CATS TO BE SAFE?

Any cat lover would say yes to the question "Do you want your cat to be safe?" However, with animals such as cats, which traditionally have come and gone from our homes as they please, safety can be a difficult issue. Owners who rate their cats' independence highly have to balance the risks of going outdoors with the value they place on their cats' right to free choice of lifestyle.

For some people, even the tiniest risk to their cat's safety is something that they cannot accept and for them, a cat must be kept inside all the time. This will remove some, but not all, of the risks of injury for cats. True, an indoor cat cannot end up in a fight with a cat that is infected with feline immunodeficiency virus (the cat version of HIV) but, cats being cats, it can get itself into mischief indoors too – see table below. When we look at the table of outdoor and indoor risks, it is interesting that the outdoor risks are all associated with safety and health; the indoor risks are more associated with behavior.

| INDOOR RISKS: | OUTDOOR RISKS: |
|---|---|
| Behavior problems because of boredom or frustration | Injury from other cats, dogs, people, etc. |
| Fear of change – overreaction to change in eating or a new food | Poisoning – directly from prey that has been poisoned |
| Obesity through lack of exercise | Disease contracted from other cats |
| Overdependence – becoming too reliant on owner | Infestation with fleas or other parasites |
| Dangers within home – getting stuck in washing machines, etc. Poisoning from houseplants | Loss – shut in sheds/cars, etc. |
| Escape – not streetwise | |

Take, for example, the question of poisonous plants. A cat with access outdoors would be able, if it wanted, to sample just about any and every poisonous plant it wanted, from those available inside, to those in all the yards in the area. However, such poisonings are rare in outdoor cats. The indoor cat is another matter, and will often nibble on potted plants that normally it would not touch, such as the very poisonous Dieffenbachia, or dumb cane. The reason for this is probably that outdoor cats have access to a wide range of grasses that they do nibble, especially, it seems, if they have digestive upsets. Thus, if they feel the need, they can find and select suitable nontoxic plants that will do what they need in terms of digestion or being sick (we are not really sure exactly what happens in the cat's digestive system and why small amounts of vegetation are important). An indoor cat may not have the right vegetation available to it and may be driven to try and find a suitable substitute – sometimes with serious consequences. Thus, the owner of a cat with access outdoors will not have to worry about indoor plants; the owner of an indoor cat will have to be very careful about what the cat has access to. Likewise, the entry for behavioral problems on the indoor cat side of the table could be quite wide-ranging – indoor cats may become frustrated and bored and problems can arise (see chapter 10). Thus, we must look at mental as well as physical dangers for our cats when we are choosing their lifestyle.

For some owners who live in very built-up or dangerous areas, or right on a road where it is highly likely that cats will get run over, having a cat that will survive outdoors is a long shot, and they may choose to keep one indoors. Later on in this book we will discuss the question of whether a cat should stay in and, if it does, what more owners should be doing to keep it healthy.

Another aspect of safe cat keeping is identification. If cats do go outside, owners often want to be able to identify them so that they can be returned if they become lost or injured on the road.

There are various forms of identification that can be used, such as microchipping, tattoos, or a collar with an address tag or phone contact.

Collars in themselves can pose a risk for cats – some years ago it became apparent that a few cats were becoming caught up by the collar as they climbed or went through the undergrowth and were actually strangled by the collar. Feline welfare organizations suggested that elastic collars would be the answer – the elastic would stretch and allow the cat to wriggle its way out of the collar. It has become evident now that perhaps this advice caused almost more trouble than the collars that did not stretch. A survey carried out by the Feline Advisory Bureau, as well as surveys done by other organizations, has found that collars which can stretch may indeed allow the cat to escape if it becomes hung up by the collar; however, they also allow the cat to get its front leg through and become stuck. There have been many very nasty injuries to an area equivalent to the human underarm where collars have cut into a cat's flesh. These injuries can be very difficult to heal because it is an area that is moving all the time. Even if the cat is not injured, its accident can be very frightening for both the cat and the owner who finds it; the cat will probably find that it cannot get home because it is unable to walk. Collars may also stretch so much that they get caught in the mouth or stuck on the teeth – again a very frightening experience that could produce serious injuries if the cat is not found and rescued. Some manufacturers have come up with a better design for collars – a snap-open variety that comes apart if the collar is pulled. These do seem a much better idea, even though the cat may go through a few more of this kind of collar because they open and get left at the scene of the tangle.

I certainly wouldn't advocate wearing a collar simply for decoration or to keep away fleas. There are other ways of controlling fleas that are more effective and do not add the risks associated with collars.

The question of whether bells worn on cat collars are effective in helping to cut down the numbers of birds killed by cats is currently being investigated by the RSPB. The evidence so far is inconclusive: some studies report that there is little effect; others report that wearing a collar with a bell does coincide with the cat catching less prey. Once again, the benefits and the risks need to be measured. If wearing the safest possible collar with a noisy bell attached does stop cats catching birds, then perhaps the small risk of associated problems is worth it.

Microchipping is definitely a good idea. A rice grain-sized chip can be inserted under the skin very easily and provides an individual code for the cat that is readable using a handheld reader. Most larger rescue centers now have one. However, if the cat is killed on the road or it gets lost in a new neighborhood, it is unlikely that it will be checked for a microchip, and the owner may never find out what happened to the cat. Cats that wear collars do look as though someone owns and loves them and are less likely to be "rescued" for simply walking around – and, if they are found dead, the owner has much more chance of being told. So, as you can see, even the identification issue can be a difficult one with cats.

In summary, cats do not make things easy – their independent and very active lifestyle can be risk-laden, and options for their safety are not straightforward.

# HEALTH

On average, cats now live longer than they did, for example, thirty years ago. Advances in the quality of food and health care we provide can mean that cats live well past the average of about 14 years old. What can we do to make sure they stay as healthy as possible?

## i) Neutering

Neutering removes much of the motivation for fighting and roaming in male cats. In this way, it cuts down on the transfer of disease through biting and, if the cat is wandering less, it reduces the chances of it crossing dangerous roads. An un-neutered male is unlikely to live long – sometimes as little as two or three years, but probably more commonly five or six years – as it has a high-risk lifestyle. Similarly, neutered females do not have the risks and trials of pregnancy and kitten rearing. Neutered ferals can live into double figures and, as we have mentioned, neutered pets may now have a life expectancy of more than 14 years.

## ii) Vaccination

The subject of vaccination is in the media a great deal these days. Worries over the MMR injection for children and other related issues – such as vaccination and Gulf War syndrome – have made people wary. However, we are looking at the problem from a very privileged position – one in which most cats are not suffering or dying from cat flu or enteritis because of vaccination that has already taken place. Vaccination is vital to the health of our cats, both individually and as a population. Just which vaccines a particular cat has and how often it has them should be looked at for that individual cat and discussed with the vet. Some indoor cats are very unlikely to even come into contact with certain diseases; others which go out are at much higher risk. Providing protection is vital to the health of our cats.

### iii) Preventive care – worming and flea treatment

Treating our cats for fleas and worms is becoming easier and easier. Manufacturers are now producing formulations that are simple to administer. Gone are the sprays loathed by all cats, and even tablets (not easy to get into many cats) are being replaced by topical treatments that are simply put on to the skin at the back of the neck. Keeping cats parasite-free will help their overall health and well-being.

### iv) Feeding

The choice of cat foods available today can be quite overwhelming. However, there are many very good quality foods around and they provide a balanced healthy diet for our cats. We need not fiddle around with homemade diets, which can often be deficient in nutrients the cat needs, unless owners are very careful about what they are doing. For cats that go outside, there is the opportunity to top off with small prey such as mice, or to scoot around the corner and eat the food left out for a neighboring cat. However, for the totally indoor cat, this is not possible and it is therefore even more important for the owner to get the cat's diet right.

### v) Good veterinary care

Veterinary care for cats is improving all the time. There are now vets who specialize in cat medicine and veterinary practices that are feline only. Good care is available for cats and it is up to owners to find a feline-friendly practice near them. Referrals to specialists for difficult cases are also a possibility. As with any problem, early investigation and diagnosis should improve the chances of successful treatment.

# FITNESS

Cats seem to stay very fit without trying very hard. Even well into their teens they can sleep for five or six hours and then get up, stretch, and jump on to the wardrobe from a standing start – no warm-ups required. They maintain their suppleness well and don't seem to suffer from the same arthritic problems as dogs, or at least not as early in their lives as their canine cousins seem to.

One of the most common problems threatening our cat population today is the same as that for the human population – obesity. Cats are getting fatter. Historically, cats have been very good at maintaining their body weight within normal range for a fit and healthy animal, and they don't get fat very often. The level of calories we provide for cats in our homes can be controlled very easily – we open the packets or get the can opener out; cats are clever, but they can't yet put the groceries away and fill their own bowls. Of course they can, if allowed outdoors, visit the neighbor for a snack or catch their own. However, a cat going out to catch some dinner will be an active one and therefore, much less likely to be suffering from a surfeit of calories.

Obese cats are usually middle-aged – the youngsters keep up an active lifestyle and very old cats tend to become thin rather than overweight. Middle-age spread on a cat tends to build up under the tummy in the area between the back legs and can hang like an apron or skirt. Some breeds, such as Burmese and Siamese, can look quite slim, but have a large store of fat around their middle.

Lifestyle is also a factor. Cats with access outdoors, and which enjoy hunting and patroling the neighborhood, will be using up energy and keeping fit. Indoor-only cats may be more sedentary. The warmth, food, and perhaps lack of stimulation are all a good recipe for more sleep and less exercise.

To summarize: we all want our cats to be happy and healthy. Sometimes steps to ensure this can be put into action relatively easily. We can ensure that our cats are vaccinated and have preventive health care, good food, and prompt treatment if they become ill. In other cases, such as the question of company, we may impose our needs, wants, or interpretations on the cat. On the issue of safety, we may want to rule out every possible risk, no matter how minor, which may lead to a very safe, but very boring existence for our cats. We need to get the balance right.

# 10

# What Cats Want

What do our cats want? It is a simple enough question, but because they cannot tell us directly, we have to guess at the answer by analyzing our cats' behavior, both as a species and individually within our homes. As we have seen, cats have strongly individual characteristics and their personalities can range from quiet and nervous to bold and demanding due to a variety of factors, including genetics, experience, and environment.

What exactly do we mean by "want"? We can look at this question on several levels. First of all "want" can be as fundamental as the basic needs of everyday life, such as food and sleep. It can also be considered under a rather more "frilly" definition, in the same sense as when we ask our children what they want to eat. The answer is not likely to be "a plate of broccoli" – more likely "several bars of chocolate" – the want takes priority over the need and is not necessarily what is best for the children themselves. Cats too will need food, but may want smoked salmon if they feel they have a choice; they may need shelter, but may want the best seat in the house next to the fire. And while there is science available for the "needs" we do have to make some assumptions for the "wants." There are some things, however, that we can feel quite confident about putting in the cat's "want" shopping basket.

Welfarists looking at what animals need on a very basic level have come up with what are called the "five freedoms." These were initially put together when looking at farm animals that rely completely upon man for their care and have no independence of lifestyle or choice. They are, however, pertinent to how we keep our pets, too. The five freedoms are:

i) Freedom from hunger and thirst by provision of ready access to fresh water and a diet to maintain good health.

ii) Freedom from discomfort by provision of a suitable environment that includes shelter and a resting area.

iii) Freedom from pain, injury, and disease by prevention or diagnosis with treatment.

iv) Freedom from pain, injury, and disease by provision of space and stimulation.

v) Freedom from fear and distress by provision of care and conditions that avoid mental suffering.

These five factors can be interpreted at the "need" end of the scale, but also at the "want" end of the scale. They provide an excellent framework by which to consider what cats do want, and then to let us add some frilly bits, too!

# FOOD AND DRINK

Our cats don't want to go hungry or thirsty, but some of them can be very particular about what they do eat!

As discussed earlier, cats have special requirements nutritionally in that they must have meat in their diet in order to obtain certain nutrients. Dogs are omnivores and can use vegetable matter to make certain nutrients that they require. Cats, however, need a high-protein diet (kittens need a diet containing 18 percent protein and adult cats 12 percent) compared to dogs, which need about 4 percent protein as adults. They require lots of sulphur containing amino acids, especially taurine, arachidonic acid – a precursor for prostaglandins – and vitamin A, which they cannot synthesize from carotene. They also have high requirements for thiamine and niacin. Cats have lost the ability to synthesize certain of these key nutrients and can only get them from meat – perhaps their success as predators has meant that these chemical pathways became redundant as their hunting ensured a plentiful supply of meat and they were not forced to resort to vegetable matter. Structurally, the cat's gut is typical of a carnivore and is short, reflecting the high digestibility of the cat's food.

For most pet cats which have access to the outdoors, their home diet can be supplemented with caught prey or food stolen from somebody else's house. There is an argument that cats have maintained the ability to hunt successfully because their association with humans may not have provided the quality of food they required. While cats were not highly valued as pets, but lived alongside man with a quasi-pest-killing role, they may have been given some scraps, but it is unlikely that they would have been given a diet that was nutritionally adequate for their high-quality needs. Thus, they maintained the ability to hunt rather than give up and live alongside us and rely on what was put in the food bowl. Indeed, cats kept completely indoors, or with limited access to a pen outside, are totally reliant on owner-supplied nutrients. Cats today can do this because the food we can now provide is nutritionally complete. However, many cats still exercise their hunting abilities and these hold them in good stead should they become lost or have to survive on their own for some reason.

If cats need meat, then their senses too will be adapted to meat intake – their senses of smell and taste will be sensitive to the nutrients that are in meat rather than those for other foods. Has the cat discarded the ability to discern other tastes because they are of little importance to its survival? Can cats tell the difference between mouse and vole, pigeon or sparrow? As in other mammals, taste buds on certain areas of a cat's tongue are sensitive to particular chemicals and the combination of signals from all of the areas on the tongue will help the cat to recognize a taste. It is thought that cats are sensitive to tastes that we would categorize as sour, bitter, and salty. They do not seem to be sensitive to sweet tastes. Some owners report that their cats like sweet foods such as ice cream, but it may be other factors, such as the fat content or the texture, which are also attractive rather than the sweetness. We get a pleasurable sensation that we associate with "sweetness" – cats may get the same sensation from a combination of amino acids available in certain meats which they find attractive.

Given the choice, cats will usually choose a food that has a high meat and fat content, a strong smell, a mixture of soft and crispy textures, and a temperature of about 95°F (35°C). They enjoy variety in their diet and will often try a new food or flavor in preference to one they are more used to.

Cats perceive flavors based not just on the taste of the food, but also on its texture and temperature, factors that in turn also affect its smell. We already know that the cat's sense of smell is far superior to that of humans and the smell of food is particularly important to a cat in order to get it to start eating. The perception of taste and smell will affect whether a cat finds a particular food palatable. The texture of food also affects how much the cat will want to eat it. Cats do not have chewing teeth the way we do – they make the food smaller by tearing at it or shearing it with front teeth until it is small enough to be swallowed. Cats will usually eat canned food or semi-moist food faster than dried food and will usually eat small meals now and again. This portion approach may mimic the pattern of catching small rodents throughout the day if they had to hunt for themselves. Typically, if food is available that does not go stale (e.g., dry food) cats will eat between 10 and 20 small meals during the day and night. The temperature they prefer is that of freshly killed prey – if it gets too high, they will be put off and if it is refrigerator-cold, the food may be unappealing, both because of the cold and the fact that it is likely to be less odorous at this lower temperature. These are basic but quite important aspects of feeding cats and although many cats are not "fussy," it may be useful to be able to tempt cats if they are not eating properly because of illness or injury.

Within our own homes we probably have two or three cats, all of which have different preferences for the type or presentation of food that we give them. Some may be very fussy; others take anything available and break all the feline laws by stealing sweet corn or some other vegetable the experts say they won't be interested in. Apparently what a cat likes or dislikes is determined by a culmination of the types of food it has experienced throughout its life. Cats may not take to a diet which is low in certain minerals or vitamins such as thiamine, perhaps because when eating something of this flavor previously, they did not feel well.

These are the cat's basic nutritional needs but, as all owners know, it can be a little more complicated than even this. Indeed, sometimes what the cat wants, rather like the food choices a child makes, may not be the best thing for it. Some cats become fixated on a certain food and are not willing to try anything else – it is fish or nothing, a certain type of dry food, or a certain flavor of canned food. While sticking to one type or flavor of a balanced diet is fine, just eating fish or liver is not, and could result in the cat becoming ill. Liver, for example, is rich in vitamin A, and cats fed diets containing raw liver can develop hypervitaminosis A and may experience stiffness, lack of energy, and skeletal problems – there is enough vitamin A for one day in a very small amount of liver! These cats tend to be very stubborn and will stop eating rather than go on to something else. If you want to change a cat's diet, mix in the new food with the old and keep trying with small portions so that the food is always fresh, and the smell is more appealing. Cats can very easily be put off stale food or food that does not smell.

The personality of a cat can also affect what foods it will accept. Nervous cats may not be happy with change; more confident cats will probably prefer something new.

Meat has a high water content and a cat eating a meat or canned meat diet may not seem to drink much water – this is because most of its requirement for water will come from the food. The cat has descended from a desert animal that can concentrate its urine very efficiently, and so will not need to drink a huge amount. Cats on a dry diet will need to drink more. Many cats also have their own little foibles about drinking water – some love it straight from the tap as it drips; others won't touch it unless it has sat for some time; some prefer water from the flower vase or from puddles outside. Indeed, most will drink it from anywhere except the water bowl!

Many cats cannot tolerate milk, although they do seem to enjoy it (probably because it contains plenty of protein, fat, and carbohydrate). Often cats cannot tolerate the mild sugar lactose.

Cats are usually very good at maintaining their body weight at optimum level – the preference for numerous small meals allows them to balance their intake of calories carefully. A fat hunter will soon become a thin one again if it cannot catch its meals. Recently, as we have already seen, cats have become much more prone to obesity, a problem we owners need to take seriously.

## COMFORT AND SHELTER

A cat's environment needs to include shelter and a resting place. In earlier chapters it became clear how important this part of its territory is.

A person's home is often said to be his castle; a cat's home is definitely valued as highly in feline terms. Indeed, a cat may prefer to stay with the territory rather than its inhabitants. When cats are kittens, they are attached to their mother, but as they grow, this attachment is often severed by the mother and the kittens are detached from her to fend for themselves. This attachment to their mother may be replaced by an attachment to their territory, something that can become very apparent when owners move to a new house just a few streets away, or even a couple of miles from their original home. Despite all the care and love the owners can provide, some cats are compelled to return to the old hunting grounds, despite the fact that the new owners of the house do not feed it, and may even actively discourage the cat from coming around.

Why this attachment to territory? What is so important to the cat? When we look at cats living without humans, we find that they have territories that they defend – whether they let other cats into their space depends on the food availability and, for female cats, the provision of a safe spot for the rearing of kittens. They need to feel secure in the area and be sure that their "space" will be able to support them and their kittens. If there is a bountiful supply of food around, then other cats may be allowed in the area. Provision of a secure kittening spot is very important, and well worth defending, too. Within the cat's territory may be areas that it will share with other cats and areas that are restricted to just that cat. The cat will organize its time and activities within these areas as it hunts and rests. It may even time-share some areas with other cats, leaving scent signals in the form of sprayed urine or scratch marks to ensure they do not meet.

Just because cats live in our homes and we feel they are safe, it doesn't mean that their instincts for safety and a refuge are removed. Thus, in our homes cats are still looking for a secure territory with plentiful food, but also a safe area. They may see our yards as the area where they will meet other cats. They will spray and mark outside to ensure that other cats keep their distance at certain times of the day. Similarly, just because we neuter our animals does not mean that we remove the need for a secure spot for kittening. It is interesting to note that female cats seem much more determined to guard their spot in our homes – it seems more difficult to add a new cat to a home that already has a female cat in residence. Neutered males seem much more open to accepting a new resident, perhaps because they do not feel the basic need for a safe kittening area.

Whether the inside of our houses equate to that safe nest box we cannot be sure, but it can help us to understand the upset which the addition of a new cat, either deliberately or accidentally, to a cat's home can cause it.

The sanctity of that indoor area is illustrated by the common scenario of a resident cat suddenly beginning to spray around the home. A little detective work reveals that the tom from around the corner is coming in through the cat flap when everyone is at work and eating the resident cat's food. He might even have a wander around, hiss at the resident, or spray inside, too! No wonder the cat that lives there is disturbed – indoors is no longer his sanctuary. Intruders have penetrated the castle and are threatening him inside, either visually or by leaving scents. He cannot relax any more. In many cases, such problems can be easily sorted out by closing the cat flap or giving the resident a magnetic or electronic key on his collar so that once more only he can get inside. He can then relax again.

We can all understand the need to feel secure – if hoodlums could walk in off the street, eat our food, and sit in our armchair while giving us some rather offensive language, we would not be able to relax. Even after they leave, we would be continually checking to ensure they were not hanging around outside ready to come in. Often the continual worry is almost worse than the reality, which may not be physically damaging, but shatters any feeling of security or relaxation.

When we have realized how strongly this can affect cats, we can work to ensure that they feel safe in our homes, but also that, if we want to introduce another cat, we try and follow some cat rules and begin to understand that threat may not just be physical, but may be left with signals which we, as creatures with a poor sense of smell, will miss altogether. To a cat, the smell left by another cat could be the equivalent of us finding a very threatening and abusive note inside our homes. Just how we can reduce a cat's stress is outlined in chapter 12.

While the scent of another cat entering the inner sanctum of the cat's territory may be the ultimate threat, we have to understand the importance of familiarity of smell to the cat within its own home. As a scent-orientated animal, the cat is as familiar with the smell of its home as we are with the visual representation of ours. If someone was to come in and move all of our furniture around, or change our color scheme, we might be very upset. Likewise, bringing in a new piece of furniture or carpet will not only change how the house looks to the cat, but will change the smell profile it has become familiar, comfortable, and secure with.

This is not to say that we cannot change our homes; it just means that we should remain aware of the effect such change can have. Most confident cats will adjust easily and soon come to terms with the new smell; other, more nervous individuals may take somewhat longer and be more traumatized. It also requires us to realize that the totally indoor cat may be more affected by changes because it is not used to any upset in its home – no other cats come in and it does not have a yard life, during the course of which it would live a little dangerously and would be able to get used to the scent of other felines. Its life will be very secure and probably very unchanging – any small alterations can be seen as a massive change to its lifestyle.

Changes to the cat's environment come not only in the form of other cats or new furniture – new people, including very small people who cry a lot, and smell of milk and other not-so-pleasant things, can provide change that can be seen as a threat to a cat's security. Again, most cats will take all of this in their stride, will get used to the smell of a new baby – or a new boyfriend for that matter – and will adapt accordingly. As time goes by, the baby will smell of the household and the household of the baby – they will all acquire a group smell that is familiar and reassuring. With a new person can also come a change in routine, and the adaptable cats will usually cope very well and take advantage of more people being around, or having waking times around the time everyone is in.

Finding secure places with a busy home can be quite difficult for a cat. If there are young children, dogs, or other cats that may upset it, a cat will go upward to find a safe place to rest. While most domestic cats will not go to such lengths as the leopard, which takes its meal up a tree to keep it safe from hyenas and lions, cats will go skyward to find a safe spot to snooze. The more nervous the cat, the more likely it is to enjoy its vertical space. Tops of cabinets are often a favorite and high spots can make the difference between a cat being always wary and one that can relax sometimes – this can make the difference between a cat that sprays indoors and one that manages to maintain its composure in the face of threats or interruptions from below.

We want more than secure cats in our homes – we want cats that are confident enough to drop any defensive behavior, to accept handling, and to be relaxed enough to behave like kittens with us. Feeling threatened may make a cat behave very differently in two very similar situations. For example, there is a cat that visits our household to eat. Our cats do not like it and will chase it away if they see it. This particular cat is very determined and rather stubborn and is not chased away easily. If the human inhabitants of the house meet this cat outside its own house, a few doors away, it will be friendly and interactive, even throwing itself on the ground and presenting its tummy for a rub. Try and approach the same cat in our house and it will begin to hiss and growl when humans get within a distance of about two yards (2 m). It is not safe to touch it at all. This is an example of what is termed the cat's "aggressive field." When cats are relaxed and not feeling threatened or stressed, this aggressive field is smaller than the cat – we can touch and stroke it without a problem. When the cat is feeling under pressure – as in this case, when it visits our house, which is the core territory of other cats – it is very guarded and the field widens all around it. Any intrusion into this area risks attack and will certainly elicit growling and threatening behavior. The size of the field can change in an instant and could explain why cats can suddenly become aggressive.

Some of the items in this chapter outline what cats need, as well as what they want. Comfort could perhaps be termed a "want." Cats are excellent at finding the warmest spot or the softest chair. We must remember that our cats' ancestors were African wildcats and as desert animals would have lived in a very hot climate. Cats can tolerate heat better than we can – humans cannot tolerate anything over 111°F (44°C), but cats do not mind a skin temperature of up to 126°F (52°C). Some cats will sit so close to the fire that their fur becomes singed; they may walk over a stovetop which has not cooled completely without seeming to be very worried by the heat. Perhaps this is a throwback to an adaptation to the hot climate and the hot sands of North Africa. Interestingly, the skin on a cat's nose and upper lip is very sensitive to touch and temperature. When kittens are born, they use their noses as heat detectors, following the temperature gradient to find their mother and the warmest spot snuggled up next to her – food is also available here, of course.

We can use heat and comfort to encourage shy or nervous cats to share space with us. Even the most reluctant feline may creep into a room and find a spot near the fire on a cold winter day. If it realizes that the spot on our lap is soft as well as warm, it may just pluck up the courage to sit on us, or at least next to us.

## AVOIDING PAIN OR INJURY

Of course, our cats don't want pain, injury, or disease. Body language among cats, while not complex enough to allow them to cooperate as a group as in the canine world, does give them a repertoire to avoid conflicts if necessary. Avoiding conflict prevents danger to life and limb through injury. Cats, like most of us, want a quiet life – they may fight if they have to, but would rather avoid conflict if possible. Most owners would not want to see their cat injured, but may sometimes inadvertently put cats into a position of conflict by keeping individuals together that just do not get along, or by keeping un-neutered cats in areas of high cat density, which almost inevitably means fighting and injury.

And while cats would not volunteer to go to the vet, they certainly want to feel better if they become ill or injured. In this, what owners want for cats and what cats want for themselves differs very little.

## SPACE AND STIMULATION

Most cats have free access to our homes and yards and further afield if they want, so provision of space is not really a problem. However, it can become a consideration when cats are kept indoors permanently. They need space to exercise and to be able to get away from other cats, people, or other pets if they want to. Stimulation may be an issue here too. A cat has a sophisticated sensory and motor nervous system – the means by which it sees, feels, hears, tastes, and smells the world and the way in which it uses these senses in a highly sophisticated manner to hunt and to communicate, to reproduce and to stay safe. It would be strange if it could just switch off all of this and live without much stimulation without some degree of frustration. Owners with indoor cats often apply the approach "what you don't know you won't miss." However, the situation may not be quite as simple as this. Perhaps if you have never tasted chocolate you would be spared those urges to eat a giant bar of Nestle's Crunch. However, a top predator may have instincts which drive it and which it needs to enact even though it has never been outside to hunt. Owners of indoor cats must be aware of this – every cat is different and must be monitored to ascertain what its particular needs are in this area. Some of these may be overcome by providing an area of fenced-in yard where the cats can enjoy the smells, sounds, and sights of outdoors in safety.

Cats also need space to escape and this can be provided vertically rather than horizontally. Cats that share a home, whether they can go out or not, may need to be able to get away from each other if they do not get on exceptionally well. Provision of high places can be quite a simple way to ensure that a less confident cat feels secure, and may avoid problems such as spraying.

# ABILITY TO CARRY OUT NATURAL BEHAVIORS

The last of the five freedoms incorporates care and conditions that avoid mental suffering, and this must include allowing the cat to carry out its natural behaviors. What behaviors would be listed as "natural" for a cat? These must surely include grooming, normal toileting behaviors, claw sharpening, hunting, sleeping, and being sociable if they wish.

## i) Grooming

Cats and grooming go together. Many beautiful pictures of cats depict them carrying out their methodical grooming routines. They may spend up to a third of their waking time grooming. A cat usually grooms symmetrically and systematically. It begins by using its forepaws to clean the face and behind the ears, covering each foreleg with saliva before wiping the "dirty" area several times in a circular motion from back to front. It then licks its front legs clean, moving on to the back legs and tail. Its supple body allows it to reach just about everywhere.

Cats are fastidiously clean animals – they hate it if their fur is coated with anything and will groom it off immediately. Indeed, being fastidious about their coats can actually be dangerous for cats, for it may cause them to ingest substances they would not normally eat. They are usually very careful about what they consume and most cats will not touch something that will be harmful to them. If a cat brushes past a fence that has just had creosote applied and then grooms it off, it could be affected by the chemicals, which are poisonous to cats. Likewise, licking tar or other chemicals off feet can have the same effect.

Why cats should be so fastidious while their canine cousins do not groom probably has to do with the sensitivity of the feline machine. Certain hairs on the cat's coat, including its whiskers, are very sensitive to movement and touch – these enable the cat to be highly aware of its environment as it moves through undergrowth or in the dark. If some of the hairs are stuck together or pulling as the cat walks, it may be getting false information or missing information from its environment. Grooming will also remove odors so that the cat will not be so easy to smell as it creeps up on its prey. A carefully groomed coat will enable the cat to move easily, will keep it dry, waterproofed, and free moving.

A cat that cannot keep itself clean will not be a happy cat – it will probably feel very uncomfortable. We need to consider this when we have the unhappy situation of an old or very ill cat that cannot get to its litter tray and may be lying in urine or feces. If the cat is not likely to improve, we need to consider its quality of life very carefully. The cat may want to clean itself up, but be unable to, and this will probably cause it considerable stress.

Grooming also seems to have a secondary use – it calms the cat. Cats often groom after they have been startled or have been confused momentarily. We see it sometimes in cats that tend to get overexcited when we stroke them – they grab our hands, bite or scratch them, and then jump down on to the floor, at which time they often start to groom rather industriously. This seems to calm them down, relieving tension and allowing them to collect themselves again. Grooming can actually be taken too far sometimes – some cats will start to over-groom and actually break off the hair and even lick the skin until it is sore. This behavior can be brought on by some sort of stress in the cat's environment that the cat cannot change or get away from. It begins to groom in an attempt to feel better and may indeed get something from the activity. However, this grooming can go beyond normal grooming and actually injure the cat. It seems to be a way of trying to deal with problems when there is no other way out (see chapter 11 for more on this).

## ii) Normal toileting habits

Cats are also fastidious about their toileting habits. Mother cats have to lick the ano-genital area of their new kittens to make them defecate and this is then eaten so that it does not soil the nest and cause conditions that are likely to provide the right environment for infections to take hold. As kittens grow they will leave the nest in order to urinate and defecate and will watch their mother and copy what she does. Thus, from day one they are being taught not to soil the den. As they grow, they will learn to dig a hole, deposit urine or feces, and cover it up again. The reason for this is probably to keep the smells covered under the ground so as not to attract predators or give information to other cats in the area. When we transfer this digging and covering behavior to our homes by providing litter trays, we must remember that cats will not want to use a dirty litter tray. Some cats may only use a tray once before they want a clean one. Others will use it a couple of times, but will look elsewhere if it is very dirty. If we try to disguise the smell with deodorants or scents, this may put off the cat even more.

### iii) Claw sharpening

As mentioned earlier, stropping or sharpening claws has two functions. The first is to pull the blunt layer of the old nail off to reveal a new pointed claw – a vital weapon for the hunting cat. The action of scratching also leaves a scent mark – whether the two are actually able to be separated, or whether the cat means to do both at once, we do not know. But it is a behavior cats need to express and they need somewhere to do it. Their choice of scratch post will depend not only on the texture of the post, but also its position. Wood is a favorite because the cat can get its claws into the surface to the right depth and pull downward, but carpets are also appreciated! We think that cats may scratch in front of other cats as a way of asserting themselves and they may choose places that are strategically useful as marking spots. This is usually outside, but can also take place within the house. Favorites are arms of chairs or couches, stairs, and carpets in general. It is probably a very satisfying feeling to get it just right! They will also use scratch posts provided by us – sometimes they need a little encouragement to use them, for example by adding some of the marker scents which will then degrade and tempt the cat back to top them up. This is easily done by gently taking the cat's paws and pulling them down in a mock scratch down the post. Doing this over a period of a couple of days should scent-mark the post and give the cat the idea of what it is for. Whether or not you provide a specific scratch post, cats will often scratch in the house. It can be very annoying, but as one of the cat's natural behaviors, it is one we have to accept and direct if we can.

## iv) Hunting

Cats are designed and made to hunt. (Chapter 5 outlines how they go about it.) Mother cats start to teach their kittens what hunting is all about very early on, bringing home injured prey when the kittens are about four weeks old so they can practice this skill. Good hunters usually have mothers that are hunting experts. Cats will hunt whether they are hungry or not – the areas of the brain that control hunger and hunting are different and are stimulated by different things. Whether cats stay in or go out, they will need to exhibit their hunting behaviors – some cats more than others. Owners must be aware of this and if the cat is not doing it for itself outside, then they must play and provide mock hunts for the cat. Cats are only usually successful in about 10 percent of hunts – they need to eat about 10 rodents a day, which means a lot of hunting. Owners of indoor cats take note – physical and mental stimulation will be part of the job of looking after an indoor cat.

## v) Sleeping

Cats are one of nature's best sleepers – they rest for about half of the day in a mixture of catnaps and deeper sleeps. If there is one thing cats have an instinct to find, it's a warm spot; indeed, it is pretty difficult to keep a cat off a hot spot. Cats love snuggling under comforters, curling up on the laundry, lazing in the warmth next to radiators, or just following the sun around the house as it warms different windowsills.

If you have ever watched your cat in the winter when it lies next to the fire, you can actually use it to judge the temperature of the room. Apparently the degree of curl with which the cat lies decreases as the temperature increases. Thus, while it is only mildly warm, the cat may curl up with the nose tucked in toward its tail. As it warms up, it uncurls and begins to lie in a flatter shape. When it gets very warm, it will lie flat out or even on its back, its legs spread out. The depth of sleep also affects the cat's position – during a light sleep its eyes may only be half closed and its head balanced on its chest. For a deeper sleep the cat lies down. In deep sleep the cat is so relaxed it must lie stretched out flat or curled up in a doughnut shape.

We humans follow a 24-hour rhythm in which we sleep and wake at fairly regular times. Cats follow a more fragmented pattern. Instead of one large period of sleep, and wakefulness during the rest of the time, they drift in and out of sleeping and waking cycles throughout the day and night. The periods of wakefulness may depend on different things – hunting patterns, patterns of its owner, or other elements in its environment. A confident cat doesn't usually worry too much about where it sleeps – somewhere in the sun or near a source of heat is preferable. The more nervous cat may need to seek out somewhere it feels safe before it will make the transition from a nap to a deeper sleep. Newborn kittens spend 60 to 70 percent of their time asleep. This starts to decrease when they are about three weeks old to levels of about 40 to 50 percent of the day as adults. Of course, if the cat is surviving completely on its own in the wild, then it may have to spend a great deal of its time hunting down enough prey to survive on. Older cats may sleep at least 50 to 75 percent of the time; like old people, they need to sleep more.

### vi) Being sociable

When writing about cats in general and when trying to pinpoint what they want, the wide range of individual characteristics of cats always ensures that it is difficult to make sweeping statements! This is very much the case when it comes to what cats want in terms of feline companionship. Just consider the cats you have owned and the differences between their preferences – some very obviously do not want another cat of any sort around and want to be the only cat in the household; others seem to need another feline for company. The important thing is to try and read our cats' preferences. The difficulty is that this only usually becomes apparent when we bring in another cat!

## BEYOND THE FREEDOMS – ATTENTION AND INTERACTION

Our cats enjoy attention. The degree to which they interact with us depends very much on their personality and on all the factors that affect this, from genetics to early environment. Most cats are highly adaptable and can live very happily alongside us with little attention, or in a close relationship if that is what both sides want. When cats want attention, they will seek it out and solicit it by rubbing themselves along us, making meowing sounds or little chirpy noises, running toward us with their tail held up straight or by simply plopping themselves on our laps and purring loudly! How the interaction proceeds usually depends on both sides – how we react and how rewarding this is for the cat (and vice versa). Some cats have a large need for attention and interaction and are very owner-orientated – examples of this would be some Burmese and Siamese cats. Others only need attention occasionally and when they choose.

A cat's natural diurnal rhythm is quite flexible. It is quite happy to be awake mostly in the day, but equally it can become almost nocturnal. We think of the cat as a crepuscular hunter – using the half-light of dawn and dusk to hunt the small creatures which are active at this time. Cats are often at their most active at this time – as the descendants of desert animals which may have hunted when it was a bit cooler rather than in the heat of the midday sun, this would also be understandable. This can also mean that some cats, especially young and enthusiastic hunters, are up and ready for action rather early in the morning during the spring and summer. If they have access outdoors, they are usually up and gone before we get up and this offers no problems. However, cats that are kept in at night, or those which target their people with their activity, can try and chivvy sleepy owners into getting up and feeding them or letting them go outside at the first hint of the dawn chorus in the summer!

## GIVE THEM WHAT THEY WANT?

This chapter has looked at a broad range of feline "wants," from basic needs such as food, to inherent behaviors such as claw sharpening.

Some of these "wants," then, go further than basic requirements and could be said to the "icing on the cake." Like the children choosing chocolate over broccoli, some cats have the option to have more than is simply needed for survival, or even more than is best for them. When it comes to food, we have seen that our cats are pretty good regulators of what they eat in terms of calories (although this has been changing in the past ten years or so). However, as facilitators of these "extras," we are in a position to give our cats what they want, or to refuse them. Is there any good reason not to give them what they want?

We often compare dogs and cats because they are the primary pets mankind has chosen to live with, and they live alongside us in our homes rather than in cages or outside in pens. We fit in with their way of life and they fit in with ours. With dogs, we need to walk them and control their outdoor activities so they do not become social nuisances. With cats, it is more flexible and there are few behaviors that cause problems to other people.

Our experience with dogs has taught us that it is not always wise to let our canine companions choose what they want or to dictate the interactions we have with them. Some dogs, given the chance, will begin to take the upper hand with the human family if they are allowed to, or are given the wrong signals. They can become aggressive if we then try to take back control. This happens because the dog is a pack animal – its behavioral repertoire allows it to fit into a group that works together for hunting and social interaction, such as breeding. Within this group there is a hierarchy and a dog's behavior will depend on how it fits into this hierarchy or organization of individuals. This structure is necessary to ensure that the members of the group are not constantly at each other's throats (literally!) and trying to rearrange who is in charge or who does what within the group. Our human family replaces other canines as the "pack" and how the people act, gives the dog clues as to where it fits within this pack and thus what it is allowed to do or to challenge. A "nice" family trying to treat a dog as an equal may have real problems if they happen to have a dog that takes advantage of their lack of command or inability to give direction in doggy terms. Such dogs, which may have been top-of-the-pack characters in the wild, or opportunistic dogs that make the best of the situation to increase their status, then become rather uncompromising when the family asks them to do something they do not wish to do, or when they do something the family does not wish them to do. This may be as simple as asking the dog to get off the couch or getting it to move because it is lying in the way – the dog may react with aggression because it feels that its owners do not have the "right" to ask, due to the fact that they have inadvertently given it a higher status than them in the home.

This lack of understanding, or breakdown in communication, between people and dogs, is typical of why some behavior problems, such as aggression, can occur. Thus, what dogs want is not always good for the dog or the humans caring for it.

However, with cats we do not have this problem. They are not obligate social animals – they seem to have the ability to be sociable if they want to and if environmental factors are right. This sociability extends to people, but again there are not built-in rules – because we have no overlap in social rules, it is hard to get the wrong message. Thus, there are very few behavioral problems caused by communication problems between people and cats – most occur because of environmental factors. For this reason, there are no reasons for not doing as our cats want! They will not decide to take the upper hand or take over the household. Thankfully, cat owners can "spoil" their cats as much as they like without a problem. Of course, providing too much food or giving in to feline demands for just one type of food can have consequences for the cat's health, and for this reason we must exert some control.

However, cats, being very clever animals, can sometimes manipulate a situation to be more rewarding for them. Being independent and not group-orientated creatures, the benefits will be entirely for them! These consequences are seldom dangerous; they are often a little tiring for the humans involved or happen at "inhumane" hours. For example, a cat may want to go outside at 5 A.M. because it feels active and ready to start the day – the birds are singing and it sounds as if there is lots to investigate outdoors. The owner, at first amused by the gentle tap of a paw on the face and a nuzzle and purr, gets up in case the cat is hungry. Reacting to a sign to let the cat out, the person goes back to bed and thinks nothing more of it. Training Day One has been a great success – the cat has early attention, food, and can go out in the sun – its owner is a very good pupil. The cat will now repeat the performance daily and, if its owner seems a little unwilling to leap out of bed at the first prod, will continue with renewed vigor until this happens. Cats can be very persistent and you only have to give in once in a while to provide enough reward for the cat to keep trying! Humans are bright enough to make great pets!

However annoying these training sessions, there are few if any consequences other than tiredness or annoyance. In general, giving in to our cats' wants makes us feel good and our cats reward us with attention and affection.

Interestingly, the comparison with children does have parallels in the cat world in one particular instance. Most people would agree that children who are given everything they want and who do not have parameters they can understand are not usually the nicest of human beings. They have to learn how to fit in with others and with the rules of our society. Our human childhood is long and children do have quite a few years to learn the rules.

Cats teach their kittens the rules too – these are not as complex as those for dogs, for example, because cats do not have to learn how to fit into a social group. Learning to hunt is much more important. How cats get on with other cats or different species is often decided within the first eight weeks of life, when the cat can form attachments to beings other than its mother. During its few first weeks, the kitten must learn to do as its mother tells it, but then to distance itself from her as she prepares to have another litter.

Sometimes humans take over the role of feline mother when kittens are abandoned or something happens to their natural mother. This involves hand feeding every couple of hours until the kitten is large enough to be weaned. One would imagine that these kittens would be very attached to their human carers and would have a very loving relationship with them. Interestingly, many such kittens actually turn into very nasty cats and react with aggression should their human "mothers" try to stop what they want to do – just like a spoiled child. We believe that this happens because humans can wean the kittens nutritionally, but do not have the expertise to wean them behaviorally. Kittens, like children, have to learn to deal with frustration and be able to cope in an acceptable manner when they do not get what they want – part of good parenting is to ensure this happens. Humans rearing kittens probably feed them at every visit and give them what they want, enjoying the relationship and the interaction with such beautiful little creatures. However, they fail to teach them the lessons a mother cat would do naturally, and so perhaps giving them everything they want at this stage can have consequences for the relationship. Luckily for us, most cats are raised by feline mothers and have learned their lessons before entering our homes.

# Stress and Health

In previous chapters we have looked at what makes cats into the fabulous creatures they are; what they need and they want out of the relationship with us, and what we want from and for our cats. It wouldn't be surprising to discover that sometimes these desires and emotions do not always fit together smoothly. It would be pretty miraculous if everything worked perfectly in a relationship between two different species, especially if one of those species is emotional and demanding, needy, and often irrational – and I'm not referring to the cats! What is perhaps even more unbelievable is that it works so well – in the majority of homes, cats and people live together very easily. This chapter focuses on those times when it doesn't work, when the cat is feeling under pressure – sometimes because of something directly attributable to its owner, sometimes not. Owners need to be able to pick up the clues to an unhappy cat, or one which is not feeling comfortable about some aspect of its life. Humans also have control, at least physically, over many of the factors in the cat's environment, and this can cause stress and conflict, albeit unintentionally.

Stress is a word that is used in a multitude of ways and, these days, in almost any situation. Stress can be a good thing and a bad thing – we need some stress in our lives so that we can learn to deal with challenging situations. Kittens kept in a boring and unchallenging environment will not learn how to investigate things, how to overcome fear, or how to tackle problems, because they do not meet anything new. We think that it is vital for kittens to meet new people, smells, sights, and sounds and experiences very early in life. This is sometimes termed "stress immunization." Kittens learn which strategies work to cope with problems or new situations, just as the immune system learns how to deal with a disease if it has had a chance to meet it before in a weaker form, and has already created the antibodies to fight it – vaccination, in medical terms. When kittens are only a few weeks old, their curiosity is stronger than their fear. Protected by their mom, they learn how to investigate things and find out what they genuinely need to be fearful about. As they grow, curiosity is then replaced by fear as a first reaction. The cat that has not had these early learning experiences may not be able to deal with novelty when it presents itself – this can manifest itself in a permanently anxious cat.

In the broad sense, we blame stress for the way we feel when we have to deal with situations that make us uncomfortable, unable to cope, or feel scared, uneasy, or bad tempered. And often, the finger is pointed at stress not just for the one-time situation that resolves itself quickly, but for any ongoing, unrelenting things that mount up and up, making each small item into an issue, and the cumulative total much greater than its components. Thus, a small thing that in itself is of little significance, can push us over the edge.

Stress can be blamed for just about every problem we suffer. However, it does allow us to express the way we feel when external factors and situations have an effect upon us.

Do animals feel stress? And if so, how does that stress manifest itself? If our cats seem relaxed around us and do not display behavioral problems, can we assume they are content? We would like to think so. If they are exhibiting behavioral problems, can we conclude that they are not happy with something in their environment and are feeling stressed? Not always – a cat that defecates outside its litter tray may not be feeling that it cannot cope – it may simply be that the litter tray has not been changed and it does not want to use such a dirty toilet. Thus, not every behavior that is out of context can necessarily be thought of as a product of "stress." In this case, there would probably have been a small conflict within the cat's mind – not wanting to soil its home, but not wishing to use the tray. The stress it felt was probably limited and in this case, resolved fairly easily by going elsewhere.

This is a different scenario than the cat which begins to urinate or defecate in the house while it has a perfectly clean and well-positioned tray that contains litter that it likes – something else is going on here, too. Conversely, the quiet cat may not be a happy cat. One behaviorist comments that cat behaviors are usually dominated by inhibition – they tend to shut down when they feel under pressure rather than become stimulated, aggressive, or shout about the problem! They tend to sit quietly or are subdued or depressed – they will remove themselves from the situation if possible. Most cats seen by behaviorists are either spraying or messing in the house, scratching the furniture, or, occasionally, are aggressive. It is suggested that this is only a small proportion of cats with problems and that we are missing the ones that are anxious or depressed because they tend not to cause any trouble.

However, as we learn about behavior changes in different situations, and ascertain the motivation for these changes, we do find that, limited as our knowledge of normal feline behavior and of being able to "read" our cats is, many behavior changes do seem to follow changes to the cat's life that it has not welcomed.

We do know that most factors which cause cats to feel stress are actually associated with the cat's environment, rather than its relationship with its owner. This second scenario is much more common in dogs where the human is part of the pack and the motivation is to remain part of the pack and to try and fit in with it – misunderstandings in the relationship in this case can provide a great deal of conflict for the dog, and it will exhibit certain behaviors as a result. This is not to say that the cat/human relationship is not important – it is just that environment is probably more important; the cat functions more as a part of the environment than as part of a pack. Thus, the most common causes of stress are threats to security from animate or inanimate factors – for example, other cats, household changes (such as renovation), or changes in routine. In chapter 10 we saw that the most important factor for cats was security of their environment. The most common causes of stress for cats are those that threaten their resources, mainly the sanctity of their homes and their core territory, which many cats would want to have to themselves and to remain unchanged.

As with people, what causes stress in one cat may have little effect on another. The individual may suffer from excessive stress and react in some way. However, the meaning of "excessive" varies from individual to individual and depends on several factors, such as how and when the cat met and dealt with stress as a kitten, how it learned to cope with it at the time, and the type and duration of the stress it is now experiencing.

## IMPROVING SECURITY WITH SCENTS

Behaviorally, cats cannot show their stress or emotions by using facial expressions, or by getting cross or crying, as humans do. What cats may do first is to increase types of behavior or activities that usually make them feel safe or secure. For example, some may try and leave more scent around from glands on the head and face, which make them feel secure. They may try and remove themselves from the situation – if there is a new cat in the house, they may stay outdoors more. If there is a despotic cat terrorizing the neighborhood outside, they may stay indoors much more, only popping out briefly from time to time when they have to, or when they feel it may be safe.

If the situation does not change and the stressful factor does not go away, they may increase their marking behaviors, which may be stepped up quite considerably. Instead of just using facial markers to rub and mark items in the house, they will start to scratch the furniture more in order to leave more of their own scent as reassurance. If this fails to resolve the problem, they may begin to spray indoors, leaving scent signals even we humans can pick up. Ways of making cats feel more secure are covered in chapter 12.

## OVER-ATTACHED CATS

Anyone who has owned several cats (not necessarily at the same time) will have recognized that different cats have different needs when it comes to attention and interaction. If cats can move freely between home and neighbors and friends, they may solicit attention from anyone they can find. If, however, a very interactive type of cat is left alone at home for a very long day, it may focus all of its needs on to its owner when he or she is there. Such cats can become very clingy or over-attached and move away from the "normal" to very abnormal behaviors. Such cats may become anxious and withdrawn when away from their owners and never begin to relax or explore without the presence of their owners. When their owners are there, they demand constant attention. These cats may have strange sleep patterns when their owners are away and may groom excessively, licking and chewing or sucking at the hair and skin, or even biting their nails. These are examples of "displacement activities" – behaviors that are performed out of context by animals in what is know as a "conflict" situation. It is thought that the animal is feeling emotionally tense or stressed and this activity helps to relieve it, if only temporarily.

## RESCUED CATS

We are much more aware of the way we keep cats in the rescue situation now. Thankfully, there are far fewer people who simply cram their houses full of cats in an attempt to rescue them from the street. Frankly, the cats would be better off on the street. Not only are these cats at very high risk of catching or passing on all sorts of diseases, they will feel very stressed by a situation of having to be in such close proximity to such a large number of cats from which they cannot get away. While some cats will seem to be very happy, others will be sitting quietly under a bed or hunched in a corner, trying to go unnoticed. These cats are highly stressed and become passive and depressed, and may lose interest in everything going on around them. Of course, such cats will not be causing any trouble and will probably go unnoticed, and so may well remain there for a long time.

Some work has been done looking at how cats in rescue react when housed in groups of four to seven cats. For the first few days, new cats try to escape or stare at the other cats, hissing and growling. After a week or so they calm down and are less vocal. Researchers looked at some other ways of measuring stress other than just looking at how the cats were reacting. They realized that even when the cats seemed more relaxed, they were still suffering from stress, but in a more passive and hidden manner. Over the next couple of weeks, the cats hid less, but still avoided other cats when feeding. This should give us an insight into how cats feel when we bring a new cat into the household – especially if they cannot get away. It should also help us deal with cats in the very stressful situation of rescue – a period when a cat may be changing its environment several times in quick succession – what we can do to minimize the stress, and help cats to settle in to whichever home they are in. In the last chapter we look at some of the ways we can minimize this.

## NERVOUS CATS

Earlier in this book we looked at what factors contribute to the personality of a cat. Kittens that are kept in isolation from an early age are often unable to cope with the activities of the normal world – they remain fearful and will avoid any situation that is not comfortable for them. If cats are continually faced with a stressful situation from which they cannot escape, they may even develop phobias or depression and become very unresponsive, not eating or sleeping in normal patterns. These are extreme cases, but, in general, life is hard for the anxious cat and treatment can be very difficult – in this case, prevention really is much better and easier than cure. See chapter 12 for more on this.

# AGGRESSION

Just like other animals, cats exhibit different types of aggression. While it may not matter to the person or cat on the receiving end just what type of aggression caused the attack or reaction, understanding the motivation and cause can be vital in trying to prevent it in the first place. We are happy to accept some forms of aggression in our cats: we don't mind if they chase other cats out of our yard; we understand a mother being defensive of new kittens; and we even understand that we may have had a hand in the problem when our cats grab us while we are tickling their tummies!

We know ourselves that if we are stressed, we may become much more reactive to small things – we can be very bad tempered if we feel that we cannot cope. Earlier in this book we looked at the idea of cats having a field of aggression that surrounds them. This field can be smaller than the cat itself, in which case the cat can be approached and fussed and will be quite happy. Or, it can grow considerably if the cat is feeling under threat or unhappy, so that anyone or any animal that comes within that zone is likely to be hissed at or scratched. This is an excellent way of thinking about cats and how quickly they can react if they feel threatened. If a cat is feeling agitated, it may well strike out at anything that comes near it – for this reason, it is very unwise to try and lift one of a pair of sparring cats out of the way – it may simply react and scratch or bite. Better to distract them both with noise or water and try to put some space between them.

One of the most common "aggression" problems behaviorists are asked about is known as "petting and biting" syndrome. The name describes the problem. Owners start to stroke their cat and it turns and grabs their hand, often holding with its front feet while kicking with the back ones. Cats vary in the degree of stroking or tickling required to elicit this response. Very reactive cats may react after merely having their head stroked for a short period – others are very laid back and can be tickled all over before they even think about getting upset. Some of the answer lies again with its sense of security or lack thereof. The cat has to trust you as it sits on your lap and relaxes. Accepting stroking is a learned response rather than a natural behavior and cats are literally putting themselves in our hands. Some may not have had much handling as kittens. Feelings of pleasure and relaxation suddenly conflict with feelings of vulnerability and the cat snaps back to attention and reacts with defensive aggression, grabbing the hand that is stroking it.

Occasionally, cats go beyond reactive or defensive aggression into proactive aggression. In such cases, owners remark that their cats attack them without provocation or prevent them from going to various places in the house – they may try to stop them from going upstairs, for example. Often these cats are kept permanently indoors. They watch birds or other cats in the yard and become excited. However, there is no means of getting rid of the pent-up energy or adrenaline and they become "wound up." Seeing a movement (for example, the owner walking past) may well trigger a reaction and the cat attacks. While some cats are happy with a completely indoor existence, others become very stressed – some people say it is caused by a "profound lack of visual stimuli" – i.e., the highly movement-motivated cat is suffering from a lack of stimulation. Such cats may have mad dashes around the house with very high levels of activity (such as kittens exhibit) and may become aggressive to owners.

## EATING AND STRESS

Eating is a behavior that is studied by behaviorists and veterinarians – changes in eating behavior can indicate a disease; they can also indicate that a cat is not happy in some way. Normally, cats enjoy a change in diet and will even eat a less palatable food just because it is different – they often return to the original food after a couple of meals of the new one. However, change a cat's environment and you will find that it prefers to stay with the original food – it feels more secure with something it knows.

New surroundings, such as a new house or a visit to a cattery, can reduce the amount the cat wants to eat, as can new people or new animals in the home.

If the cat needs a special diet to help it deal with a particular disease, the best idea is to introduce the change gradually while the cat still has access to its original diet (unless it is vital to change the diet immediately). In this way the cat becomes familiar with the new diet – if it is not feeling well it may have an even greater need for security and so will be loath to try something new.

Similarly, if the cat has to go somewhere else, for example to a boarding cattery, ensure that it is given a diet it knows – the familiarity of the food will lessen the stress felt at the change.

Poisoning is rare in cats. With free access outdoors they seldom, if ever, sample poisonous plants and we do not need to worry what we grow in our gardens from a feline point of view – especially since cats wander to other yards anyway and we have no control over what other people grow. However, cats that are confined indoors or in a pen, are much more likely to sample vegetation that they would not normally touch. This may be because they have a need for some plants in terms of self-medication, but these are not available in this indoor situation or are limited in a run. Boredom may also be a factor that turns their attention to the plants they would normally ignore. Whatever the reason, it is another consideration that owners of indoor cats must consider – remove anything dangerous and ensure that cats have access to grass or herbs that they can chew safely.

Some cats exhibit what is called pica – the eating of non-nutritional items – for example, some have a strange need to eat woolen garments. This trait was first documented in the 1950s and seems to be found mostly in Siamese and Burmese cats. Research revealed that most cats began by eating wool, but then progressed to other fabrics, too – some even had a taste for electric cables. Some ate or chewed material regularly, others randomly. They selected sweaters, towels, woolen furniture (including tweed couches!), or underwear. Most did not come to any harm, but some needed surgery when the "food" became an obstruction in their digestive system.

While it is always important to have the cat checked in case there is a medical cause for the problem, it is thought that eating unusual items such as wool or cotton can be a disorder of the cat's natural hunting behavior, which is to stalk, pounce, tear off feathers, fur and skin, and eat the prey. Not only do skin and feathers pass through the cat's stomach, but the cat has an instinct to do the tearing and plucking before swallowing.

Some pet cats become compulsive about this part of the predatory sequence – tearing off feathers and skin bit by bit and swallowing it all. Eating ordinary cat food gives these cats no opportunity to tear and rip, so the cat looks for this somewhere else.

Cats will tear and rip and then eat the wool, fabric, or whatever they have chosen as their "prey."

Wool eaters are often pedigree breeds kept indoors without access to prey, although not always. In the past experts suggested feeding high-fiber food, gristly meat, and making mealtimes more frequent in the hope that this would make the cats feel that their stomach was full. It would also give them lots of opportunity to chew. Now they suggest supplying something closer to nature – something for cats to tear and shred such as dead whole turkey chicks, day-old chicks, or dead whole rats and mice sold frozen by pet shops for reptiles. Other food supplies can be given in the form of dry pellets contained within a toy – the cats have to move the toy around so as to release the food – again, this gives them something to do and simulates a kind of hunt for their food. More hunting play is also suggested, giving the cat a chance to play out all those hunting expeditions it would be undertaking if it was in the wild.

## NIGHT CALLING

In the past 10 years, an interesting phenomenon has come to light in older cats. Owners find that their cat (usually more than 12 years old) starts to call out at night when the household is fast asleep. They leap out of bed to see if the cat is all right. The cat has a quick cuddle and is checked over and then happily goes back to sleep. At first owners are fearful something is dreadfully wrong with their cats; however, after having them checked over by the vet and seeming fine in the daytime, they begin to get a little less alarmed by what soon becomes regular nighttime calling. We think that older cats are feeling less secure and more dependent on their owners for that security – in the night, when alone, they suddenly feel the need for some reassurance. Owners usually oblige when the call goes out. However, it can get very tiring! The cat feels less stressed about life, but owners start to feel as if they have a baby in the house that needs regular feeding!

This is one of the ways in which our cats do actually come to us for help when they feel anxious – many times they do not, or cannot, and so we have to be able to spot the problems ourselves.

## HEALTH AND STRESS

Until very recently how we looked at our animals was divided very crisply between physical health and illness, and acceptable and "problem" behaviors. Illness was considered purely in veterinary terms and treated medically or surgically, while bad behavior was countered by punishment. However, over the past 20 years, and especially during the last 10 years, we have become aware of the motivations for "problem" behaviors, and at the same time have begun to notice the overlap between both the physical and psychological health of the animal.

Veterinarians and behaviorists are moving closer together in their fields of work and realizing that some medical problems should be interpreted in the light of the cat's interaction with its life and its lifestyle. Once ignored by the veterinary profession, it is now accepted that stress can have major effects on the health of our pets, as well as on their behavior. The effects of psychological stress are now the subject of great interest in both animals and people – often in relation to how it affects the immune system.

Stress can come in many forms – it can be sudden and short-lived, or it can be a long-standing problem. How this affects animals varies from individual to individual. It is a very complex subject, but

143

one that has raised enough interest for people to start looking for answers.

We have been aware of the detrimental effects of stress on the immune function in animals we farm (especially those we keep in high densities) and how this can impact on production. The central nervous system and the immune system communicate with each other. It may be that stress factors cause immune cells to be redistributed in some organs (such as, for example, the skin, the digestive tract, or the bladder) and affect them in the same way. These changes start to explain some of the veterinary problems we feel may be stress related in our pets.

# HIGH BLOOD PRESSURE

Some stress-related problems in cats closely resemble diseases in humans. For example, did you know that cats can suffer from high blood pressure? This hypertension, as it is known, can cause or exacerbate illness in cats as it does in people. It can result in heart problems and also result in blindness because of damage to the eye. One scientific paper written about blood pressure in cats was entitled "Evaluation of White-Coat Effect in Cats" (Belew and others, *Journal of Veterinary Internal Medicine*, 1999). White-coat effect is an accepted finding in people – in 1940 it was recognized that blood pressure and heart rate measured in a clinical setting were higher than if the readings were taken at home. This is thought to be a defense reaction in response to the stress associated with the clinical setting. Researchers measured the blood pressure of cats in a clinical environment (such as a veterinary office) and found that the same thing happened – the cats' blood pressure rose. Thus, for a veterinarian who is trying to get a blood pressure reading from a cat, it is advised that a quiet, undisturbed environment is the setting – the cat is given time to get used to its surroundings – and that several readings are taken.

To summarize: we now believe that cats probably experience the same feeling of fear and tension in a veterinarian hospital or office that humans do in similar places, and that this can result in increased blood pressure in both species.

## LOWER URINARY TRACT DISEASE

Current studies are examining a problem called feline lower urinary tract disease (FLUTD), some of which is what we would equate to cystitis in man (and more often women). FLUTD is seen quite commonly in veterinary practice – cats often strain to urinate, may urinate in strange places (for example, outside the litter tray), and may have blood in their urine. Occasionally there is complete obstruction of urination and this can be a life-threatening condition.

Anyone who has suffered from cystitis knows what an uncomfortable problem it is – in people it causes pain during urination and a feeling of constantly needing to urinate in the individual. Cats often urinate outside the litter tray – perhaps the urge to pass urine was just too great to give the cat time to get to the tray. Perhaps cats are suffering from similar types of symptoms to people. Often no cause for the disease can be found in cats – in fact, in about two-thirds of cases, there is no apparent cause. The same thing has been noted in some women, and is referred to as interstitial cystitis. It has been suggested that stress and psychological factors are among what is know as the "flare factors" for the problem – i.e., they seem to make it worse or even cause it. One theory is that stress causes changes in the nervous system, which releases neurotransmitters that can act to cause, or exacerbate, local pain and inflammation. The same may well happen in cats. A thick layer of mucus lines the bladder and protects it from bacteria and from damage from crystals in the urine. Cats with feline idiopathic cystitis (cystitis of unknown cause) have been found to have lower levels of this protective layer. While it is not known whether this defect caused the inflammation in the first place, its presence is thought to make it worse.

A recent study suggests that there are a number of factors that may be "flare factors" in cats, the most significant of which is conflict with another cat in the house. Others have included abrupt changes in diet, environment, weather, overcrowding, owner stress, or the addition to the household of new pets or people. Stress associated with urination is particularly important and may have a number of causes – for example, the cat may not like the type of litter or the position of the litter tray because it makes it feel vulnerable or exposed; it may face competition for the litter tray from other cats, or experience aggressive behavior from other cats while on the tray or urinating outside.

Another study, in New Zealand, looked at the elements that seem to influence the development of FLUTD. Being overweight and inactive were common factors. It is thought that such cats sit around more and do not empty their bladder as often as perhaps they should – the urine becomes very concentrated (a process cats are very good at anyway) and it can provide an excellent environment for the growth of crystals within the urine, or for concentration of infection or other factors within the bladder that might affect its function. In addition, many cats with this problem came from multi-cat households – could this be the stressor (the problem causing the stress)? Moving house was another common factor – again, a stressor. Interestingly, winter and the weather was also found to have an effect – cats didn't want to go out in the cold or on rainy days, and so urinated less.

## GLUCOSE LEVELS

Cats also suffer from what is known as "stress hyperglycemia" – an increase in the glucose in the blood caused by stress. This can be a problem for veterinarians trying to ascertain whether a cat has diabetes or not – simply taking one sample that shows elevated levels of glucose will not be enough to make a diagnosis – the cat may merely have been stressed by the procedure and by simply being in the veterinary office. Interestingly, veterinarians have found that it is not easy to tell which these cats are by just looking at them. Some cats, which are very stressed and almost have to be taken off the ceiling, will have normal glucose levels in the blood; others, which appear calm, can develop severe hyperglycemia. As usual, the cat makes it very difficult to judge its behavior and there is wide variation between individuals.

## SKIN PROBLEMS

Some cats suffer from skin problems such as overgrooming and an acute sensitivity of the skin. Cats with this hypersensitivity may bite or lick at themselves, the skin can twitch or even ripple, and the cats may jump up and run as if stung and seem very agitated. Cats may also become aggressive, perhaps because they are constantly aggravated by their skin and may not be resting or sleeping properly. While there can be simple causes for itchiness or sensitivity, such as allergy to fleas or other types of skin problem, for some of these cats, no cause can be found. Cats that overgroom can "self-barber" (an excellent term noted in a feline publication) by breaking off hairs or even pulling them out. They may have bald patches where they have removed all the hair, and the pattern of the baldness may be symmetrical since the cat grooms each side excessively to the same extent. This can be very extensive and may affect the whole stomach, the cat's sides or flanks, and its back, or may occur just along the outside of the thighs and the stomach. Researchers have suggested that there is a change in the nervous system in these cats and that the nerves in the skin may be stimulated, and thus cause this very sensitive reaction – it is thought that this can be exacerbated by stress. Interestingly, a few cats also nail bite, splitting and breaking the nails.

Many researchers have examined "psychogenic alopecia" (behaviorally induced hair loss) and investigated a large number of cases in great detail. In most cases, they found that there was a medical cause, such as allergy to fleas, for the hair problems. They concluded that it was actually quite a rare problem and should be kept in proportion and investigated fully before rating it as purely behavioral.

# IMMUNE CHANGES

It may be that in many of these cases the body reacts to stress by producing a change in the immune system – perhaps in anticipation of an injury so that the body is ready to react if a problem occurs. However, if the stressor does not go away and the cat is subjected to constant levels of stress, the body continues in this mode. A free-living or feral cat may be able to resolve this by removing itself from the situation – be it another cat, changes to its environment, lack of stimulation and boredom, or another reason. Cats that live with us may not be able to do so quite so easily. Those cats that have access to the outdoors may remove themselves to the yard for quite long periods when a new cat is introduced and gradually get to know and (hopefully) accept it. For cats that cannot go out or have nowhere within a house to retreat to, the stress continues. Likewise a cat that is suffering from over-attachment cannot resolve the problem if it has no access to company.

## FIP

The feline veterinary world is full of fascinating problems – cats have a unique physiology that keeps many excellent veterinary minds busy trying to ascertain just what is happening and how to solve the problems. We have now fully accepted that a cat certainly doesn't behave in the same way as a small dog, either medically or behaviorally.

One such disease that still has vets baffled is feline infectious peritonitis, known as FIP. Most cat owners will be unaware of it until they have firsthand experience.

In the most common scenario, a healthy young (usually pedigree) kitten goes to a new home and falls ill very quickly. Owners take it to the veterinarian who may have difficulty in making a diagnosis – there are no tests that can simply identify the disease. Often the cat has a large fluid-filled abdomen and a tentative diagnosis of FIP is made. The veterinarian will try and treat to ensure that all possibilities of other diseases that may have similar symptoms are covered because, unfortunately, FIP is inevitably fatal. We have not yet found a way to treat it.

In medical terms, FIP is a very interesting disease and we believe that there is a stress element to the disease. FIP is caused by a group of viruses called coronaviruses. These are ubiquitous where there are groups of cats together – a survey of pedigree cats (which are usually kept in groups by breeders) found that 90 percent had met coronaviruses and had antibodies to them (about 50 percent of mixed breeds also have antibodies). However, in the vast majority of these cats, the virus will sit in the digestive system and not cause anything more than perhaps a mild bout of diarrhea.

In some cats, for some reason, the viruses change or mutate to a form that causes FIP. The changed virus moves into the bloodstream and from there into the body organs, where it causes severe inflammation. In some cats, the inflammation of the blood vessels in the tissues lining the chest and abdominal cavity causes an accumulation of fluid that may compress the lungs and cause difficulty in breathing. In other cats, inflammation may occur in internal organs, such as the liver and kidneys, the eyes, brain, and intestines.

Just why the virus changes and what causes this we do not understand, but the common scenario of the kitten in a new home may give us a clue. This can be a very stressful time for a new kitten – it is leaving the environment it knows (remember how important environment is to cats and that they bond to the environment on weaning, transferring their bonding from their mother), and the cats and humans it knows, and going to a completely new situation. We think that the immune system in kittens is not fully mature and that during this stressful period, either the virus changes in line with the stress affecting the body, or that if it has changed to this more virulent form, the immune system cannot cope with it and the virus goes on to take over the body.

It is hard to explain such a complex disease here. Suffice it to say that stress seems to be a strong factor in the transition of a harmless coronavirus in the digestive system to a pathological coronavirus in the cat's body. Let's hope that research into the disease comes up with something with which to combat it.

The study of how stress affects our pets is a relatively new area. We know it affects behavior and now are beginning to be able to pinpoint some of its effects on health. The above examples may be joined by many more as our knowledge improves. Measuring stress is not straightforward – there are biochemical parameters we can measure, but none give a direct answer – we must combine all the methods we can to pick up the clues to how our cats are feeling and to help them if they are suffering. This should become a joining of veterinary and behavioral studies as both disciplines can feed into and learn from the accumulated knowledge, applying it to help cats recover physically as well as mentally. Pet owners too can pick up the signals if they know what to look for and what to avoid.

# 12

# Getting the Balance Right

In chapter 11 we looked at some of the problems that cats have which we feel may be associated with stress or conflict. Conflict in this sense means conflict within the cat, rather than between cats, although aggression between cats can indeed be one of the major causes of stress.

The aim of this chapter is to look at ways in which we can understand and minimize the stress some cats may be experiencing. As explained before, the majority of cats are probably very happy and relaxed in their households. However, some trends of ownership are pushing them into situations in which some cats will not be happy.

## UNDERSTANDING AND RESPECT

The first thing we can do is to understand and respect the cat for the animal that it is, not what we want it to be. In chapters 3, 4, and 5

I have tried to explain how the natural cat behaves. Of course, cats have lived closely with mankind for thousands of years and in some ways it is difficult to remove humans from the equation; however, given minimal human input, cats choose to behave in a certain way and we must be aware of this. The cat is a finely honed hunter and has many innate behaviors connected with this primary activity. We must not deny this aspect of our cats – the way they look and act is a function of this hunting ability.

The cat has already shown how adaptable it can be. It lives in regions that vary from subantarctic islands to deserts, from desolate regions to dense cities. It can live alongside us with very little human input, or in an intensely one-to-one relationship with its owner. There is no doubt our lifestyles have changed, and our cats' lives have changed along with our own. The reality of today's society is that we live much faster and have greater expectations of what we can do and how we can control our environment, including our pets. Pressure is on us to earn more money to pay bigger mortgages and to have possessions and homes that go with a certain standard of living. This means all the adults in the household have to work and must have more control over their lives in order to keep abreast of everything that is going on. The ever-adaptable cat fits in well with this, but we are in danger of forgetting it is an animal, with special needs that are not swayed by the pressures we have on us. Not only do we forget it is an animal, we do not even realize just what a fantastic animal it is.

Perhaps only 10 years ago people would have been very amused to hear of a cat with "behavioral problems" – cats simply weren't considered in this way. Now we accept that our pet felines do indeed sometimes exhibit behaviors that we do not find acceptable in our homes. We now have enough knowledge to try and tackle them and to ascertain just what it is that is causing our cats to behave in this uncharacteristic way.

The kinds of behaviors we are considering are spraying and marking in the household, aggression between cats and toward people, overgrooming, nervousness, and depression. There may not be only one cause of the problem and for some cats, a certain lifestyle just doesn't suit their personality. Whereas one cat may be happy jostling for position in a house full of other felines, another will spend its life hiding in the corner; while one cat may be happy to laze away its days in the comforts of a permanently indoor environment, another may go crazy trying to get outside. These are not hard and fast rules, just ideas on how to pick up that there is a problem and perhaps how to overcome it.

## CHOOSING THE RIGHT CAT

One of the first areas to look at is how we choose our cats, how we socialize them and how we expect them to fit in with our lives.

As outlined earlier, most of us choose a cat or kitten because of its coat pattern, a preference that is often influenced by a cat we had as children, or one which friends had. We may also be influenced by the media – currently both silver tabbies and Bengals, both of which have spectacularly beautifully marked coats, are used in a variety of advertisements and their popularity is growing rapidly. The rise of the popularity of the Persian may have had something to do with a certain carpet advertisement that featured a glamorous and elegant white, fluffy feline lying gracefully on said carpet to suggest luxury and softness. People who think they might like a cat will be tempted by these images of beauty. Not that there is anything wrong with wanting a beautiful cat (or perhaps we should say a more beautiful cat). However, this popularity brings with it an increasing demand on breeders to produce kittens, and there will always be unscrupulous people ready to take advantage of a demand in order to make money. There are excellent breeders of cats, but there are also awful ones. The average person who has never bought a pedigree kitten can easily be persuaded to take a kitten that may not be well, or may not have been socialized properly, because it was mass-produced and did not have the time and attention required to ensure its health, both physically and psychologically. Both of these scenarios can produce cats that are not confident with life and for which living in a busy world can be very stressful.

Kittens need to meet novel situations, people, and objects when they are very small – between three and seven weeks old. If they are mass-produced in a situation where they are kept in an unstimulating environment at this time, such as a yard shed or even a specially built structure, they are unlikely to have met everyday situations during this period. If a breeder has several litters of kittens at a time kept outside and is also working, he or she may not have the time (or the knowledge or expertise) to understand the effort that is required to ensure that kittens are well-balanced and confident with life. Nervous kittens will not make good pets.

Most people want a cat that is friendly, confident, and joins in with the family and other pets, if they have them. Here are some ways to avoid the pitfalls.

## BUYING A PEDIGREE CAT

Do your homework. Find out about the breed you want and whether the general characteristics and behaviors it is said to have will suit your lifestyle.

If you do not have time to groom a cat every day, do not consider getting a Persian (categorized as a longhair); you may not even want to consider a semi-longhair (for example a Birman or a Maine Coon), which will still need some grooming. A Persian will *not* be able to look after its coat on its own – it will need you to help. In order to do this, you will need to start grooming the kitten every day as soon as you get it – even if its coat is not yet very long. In this way, the cat gets used to it and accepts it as a normal way of life. You will have to learn how to do it and what equipment is necessary. A good breeder will help you and give you advice on what is appropriate – find out first.

If you want your cat to be independent and not live in your pocket, perhaps you should not be considering the more interactive breeds such as the Siamese or Burmese or the Rexes. These will demand attention, are likely to be rather noisy, and may get bored if you do not provide stimulation for them – these are not low-maintenance cats either. However, if you do want something interactive and even dog-like, then they may be for you. If you do not want an active outdoor cat, the breeds such as Maine Coons may be best avoided.

Ask the breeder about the breed, but try and do your own independent research, too. Some breeders will be very honest about their breed and the particular characteristics of the cats they breed. They will not want to sell to you if they do not feel you and the cat will fit well together. Others may just want to sell a kitten, not minding to whom and to what circumstances it goes. On the other hand, some breeders are very prescriptive and may not sell a kitten to a home where it would be allowed outside, or are very dogmatic about the diet the cat should have. If you have not found out anything for yourself, you will not know which of these scenarios you may be in! One way to do this is to go to a local or national cat show and talk to the breeders and other owners there – get a broad view from a number of people. It will probably become evident who is being sensible and who might be able to point you in the right direction. You can also see the cats in real life and find out the characteristics of the breed.

Anyone can become a "breeder," you just need to be able to put two cats together at the appropriate time. The good ones know a great deal about the health and behavior of cats and can pass good information on to you.

Likewise, be careful about health. Good breeders will ensure the kittens are healthy and have been vaccinated before you can take them home. They will be around 13 weeks old by this time. Check for yourself, too. Don't take on a kitten that has a runny nose or runny eyes or an upset stomach. Do not be taken in by stories of kittens scratching each other in the eye (hence the runny eye), or feel sorry for the kitten. If you are happy to take the risk that the kitten is not very healthy and accept the subsequent veterinary bills (and probably some heartache), then go in with your eyes open; some people just cannot resist taking a sickly kitten home to get it out of bad circumstances, or because they feel sorry for it.

When you do go to visit the breeder, look at the health of all the cats there. If there are lots of cats and kittens everywhere and the place is not pleasant to be in or smells unpleasant, then there is a strong chance that the hygiene is not good and disease may be rife. It is best to keep cat numbers down to ensure that they can be managed and socialized properly and that disease risk is kept to a minimum. Be prepared to leave without a kitten before you go – most of us (and I am equally guilty on this, having done it once myself) want to go home with a kitten. We do not want to wait another day; however, we may take on one which is not healthy, will cost a lot to make well, will cause heartache, may never be a confident pet, or may bring home disease to our other cats. Sometimes it may just be that the cat stays nervous and never makes the kind of pet we want. This kind of cat is often the one which objects very strongly to us getting another feline, and so we are left with one cat for the next 14 years, which is not really what we wanted.

Another factor in getting a very attractive pedigree cat is that people worry that if it goes out, it will be catnapped or stolen. For this reason, they keep it in indoors. If they had chosen a mixed breed, this fear would not have been a factor and they would have let it go outside. In this case, it is time to think about the cat's feelings. Mixed breeds are just as beautiful and graceful as pedigrees. Why not get a common house cat that you are happy to allow a rich and varied lifestyle and which you can enjoy without the worry?

## TAKING ON A MIXED BREED

Mixed breeds come from various different backgrounds – often from "accidental litters" produced because people have just not gotten around to neutering their kitten, or from rescue centers. Again, these are some basic guidelines.

A cat from a rescue center is indeed in great need of a home. But be careful about the type of environment you get it from. Like breeders, rescues can vary dramatically in their quality. The good ones keep cats in separate pens with runs in a clean and friendly environment. They will be organized and the hygiene will be excellent. The bad ones will have rooms full of cats all lumped in together and will be disorganized and very unhygienic. Just because the people who run rescues have their hearts in the right place and like cats, does not mean that they are doing a good job. As with anything, knowing how to do something well takes knowledge and experience. Managing a large number of animals successfully to keep them in a happy and healthy state actually takes great organization and discipline – just liking cats and wanting to do good is not enough. Again, choosing the wrong source for your kitten could mean you end up with one that is not healthy.

Just as breeders need to spend time socializing their kittens and getting them used to "real life," so do rescue facilities. It may be more difficult to let kittens learn about life in a rescue because they are confined to a pen – rescuers will have to work extra hard and spend plenty of time handling the kittens and introducing new toys and situations.

Sometimes the kitten from the "accidental" litter is the best bet of all for getting a well-rounded and confident cat. Often the mother cat has the kittens in the house in the midst of various adults and children, dogs, and other creatures. The kittens sample lots of different people and all the everyday goings on, such as vacuuming and cleaning, televisions and doorbells, noise and activity. They will go to their new homes thinking all of this is perfectly normal and will be able to cope with just about any situation that is thrown at them.

## MATCH YOUR NEEDS

Whether you are going for a pedigree or a mixed breed kitten, it may be very useful to match your needs to that of the source of the kitten. If you have dogs or children, try and find a source where these are already part of the kitten's life. If you have a noisy and active household, try and find a kitten that is used to this already and will simply slot in without being scared to death by a lifestyle so completely different from the one it has so far experienced. Ask about handling and where the kittens are kept – do they see people? Ask about the mother and if you can see her for yourself – a confident mother who is happy with people will be passing similar messages on to her offspring.

# PROVIDE SOME CONSISTENCY TO THE CHANGEOVER

Going to a new home is a huge change for a kitten – it leaves its mother and the only place it has known and enters a new world that smells, looks, and sounds very strange. Within this context, try and minimize the stress of all the "newness" by (initially anyway) sticking to the same food and litter that the kitten has been used to. Bring a blanket or old T-shirt or piece of bedding from the original home so that the kitten has something that smells familiar. Put this in the kitten's bed for reassurance.

# HOW CAN ALL OF THIS HELP?

In many cases of behavioral problems, prevention would have been a lot less painful than cure. Indeed, in some cases it may prove impossible to overcome the inadequacies of the kitten's very first two months of life. For example, a very nervous cat may never enjoy being in the company of more than its owner, and even this confidence may take many years to build up. It must be very stressful to live a life frightened of every movement or sound going on around you. It is not very rewarding for most owners either.

If you can match your new kitten to your household needs, then you stand a much better chance of getting a cat or kitten that will be happy there. If it is healthy from day one, that can only be good, too. Don't underestimate how much hair is shed by a long-haired or semi-long-haired cat – if you are a fastidious housekeeper, it will bring more work and perhaps some aggravation. If so, perhaps a short-haired cat would be better for you.

Another scenario where some forward thinking will help is where the cat is going to be an indoor cat – it will not have access to the outdoors for various reasons that have been outlined earlier in this book. In this case, owners often feel very guilty that their cat is getting bored or lonely if they go out. However, introducing a new cat to an indoor-only cat can be difficult and owners don't want to risk upsetting the cat, too. The answer is to get two kittens from the beginning. Littermates usually get along well – they have formed attachments during their early sensitive period and are more likely to get along than kittens that are not related or adult cats brought together.

## GETTING ANOTHER CAT

As I have been at pains to point out in this book, the cat comes from a solitary-living ancestor, but it can be sociable if it wants to, and if the circumstances are right. Cats too are very individual characters – what suits one may not suit another.

Cat lovers enjoy their cats and they often want to have more than one. In terms of time, space, or energy, having two cats makes very little difference to having one – the cost of food and veterinary treatment will be doubled, but that may not be a problem. How will you know if your cat would like a friend? You may not. Your cat may have lived with another cat, but that does not guarantee that he will get along with another cat you bring home. There is not really anything to do but try. The important thing to realize is that you are getting another cat for you, and not necessarily for the good of your resident cat. He or she is very likely to be happy with the single cat arrangement as it is!

However, if you do want to go ahead, then again planning is important. What age or sex should you get? How should you introduce the two cats to each other? These factors will all have a part to play in the successful integration of the new cat.

When it comes to the age of the new cat you are getting, it is probably true to say it is easier to introduce a kitten than it is to introduce a new adult cat to a household. Kittens pose less of a threat and are much less reactive themselves, responding with play rather than by becoming aggressive in the presence of the resident cat – thus, they do not escalate the tension by adding to it. They are not mature and do not pose such a threat initially.

Which sex of kitten to choose is also an interesting question. Anecdotally, it seems that female cats are much more defensive of their territory than neutered males. This would be understandable in the context of wanting to have a safe core area for the bringing up of kittens. Just because cats are neutered does not mean that they lose this instinct – neutered females are in the same hormonal state as females that are not in season; they may thus still behave in a similar fashion. Neutered males seem to be more open to letting other cats into the household – they are in a different hormonal state than the entire male and perhaps do not feel the need to be so defensive about the area. That said, they are territorial animals and will not take kindly to a new cat in the area, initially anyway. If the resident cat is female, it may make sense to get a male kitten – remember the feral cat scenario in which female cats chased away other females pretty fiercely, whereas they let males come and go. Neutered males may be happy (eventually) to accept either sex – individual characters excepted, of course!

## MAKING INTRODUCTIONS

Just how you introduce a new cat to the household can also make a difference to the levels of stress. You can do quite a lot to ease the new cat in. This is where it is important to remember what is important to cats – security of their core territory from the presence and smells of other cats. Getting a new cat will violate this quite considerably!

First of all, choose a quiet time – not Christmas or when you have a houseful of guests or visiting children. Have everything ready for the new cat so you can work smoothly and quietly. Whether you are introducing an adult cat or a kitten, the principles are the same.

The first thing to try and sort out is the scent problem. It would be better if, when your resident cat first sees the newcomer, its scent is already familiar. Thus, while it might be tempting to just bring the new one in and "let them sort themselves out," this can lead to chases and aggression and a situation that is very difficult indeed to resolve. Bring the new cat into the house and put it in a separate room. Settle it down with something that smells familiar to it, and give it a tray and food. If it seems to want cuddles and attention, then give some; if it needs a little time to explore and relax, leave it for a while. When you return to it, bring food or a tidbit so that your presence is associated with something good. Stroke the cat and then go and stroke the resident cat, beginning to mix their scents. Wipe the new cat with a soft cloth, especially around the head area where the glands that produce pheromones are situated. Dab this around the house – you will not be able to see or smell anything and may feel a little ridiculous – however, watch the resident cat take note of the smells, and you will be reassured you are doing something useful. Stroke your resident cat and mix that scent by stroking the new one. In this way, you start to integrate the smell of the resident cat and the house on to the new cat and vice versa. You can swap the cats around so that they get to smell the parts of the house that the other one was in. However, don't let them meet for about a week. By this time the new cat will feel a bit more "at home" and the resident will have become familiar with the new smells; indeed, it will be smelling of the new cat itself.

However, it is still not time to "let them sort themselves out." The best approach to letting cats see each other while preventing any type of confrontation is by using a kittening pen or dog crate. Dog crates are often used in the back of cars to keep dogs where they are supposed to be. Kittening pens are about the same size and often used by breeders to house cats with kittens within the home. It provides a den and enables them to keep the cat and kittens safe. These pens are usually made out of metal or plastic-coated metal and are about $3^1/_2$ feet (1 m) high by $2^1/_2$ feet (0.75 m) deep by $3^1/_2$ feet (1 m) wide. The door can be open or shut securely. It provides ample space to provide a bed (a cardboard box with a cozy blanket or an igloo type of bed will give the cat a feeling of safety, rather than being exposed) as well as a litter tray. You can put a blanket over the top to increase the feeling of security if you need to – depending very much on the cat or kitten. Use this to provide the new cat or kitten with a den as soon as you get it. After a week or so you can move the pen to the kitchen or another room more in the hub of the house. The new cat will be familiar with the pen and will then have to get used to the new position. This is when you can start to let the cats see each other. Within the pen, the new cat is protected and secure. There will probably be a certain amount of hissing and growling and the resident cat may simply run outside. However, he will return (especially if you tempt him with some favorite food). The cats can watch each other and can even sleep in the same room (one in the pen) and so get used to each other. Obviously, you can let the new cat out when the resident is outside or shut in a different room. When you think they are tolerating each other quite well, you can open the cage and let the new cat out. Leave the cage there as a refuge. In fact, if you have a new kitten, the cage is excellent for allowing you to go out and know that it is safely shut inside with food and a litter tray, rather than getting itself in trouble in the house (kittens are notorious for finding some way of getting stuck on or in something). Most cats are very happy inside for periods of time.

The cage is also an excellent way to coax nervous cats to integrate into the household. The pen can be placed in a room where it is relatively quiet, but where there is some activity and the cat has to watch proceedings while still feeling safe inside. Very nervous cats would have run off and hidden under the bed just in case there was life-threatening danger (if you are a nervous animal everything is life-threatening). From under there they never learn that in fact there is no danger and it is actually quite nice being able to observe what is going on and get choice morsels of food from your owner for just sitting there! Once the cat seems more relaxed with this room, you can move it to a place of greater activity so that it can get used to that, too. The pen can eventually be opened and the cat can go in and out as it pleases. The pen can be used to introduce dogs too – it ensures safety, but allows meetings.

If you can't get hold of a pen or crate, then you can use a cat carrier or basket for initial introductions. Obviously, you can't use it as a den or base because it is too small – however, it does allow the cats to meet in safety. Place the new cat or kitten in the carrier and place it on a coffee table or a chair. In this way, the cats are not on the same eye-level and it is harder for them to make aggressive eye contact. Let the resident cat come in and praise both cats and reward them with food (they may not be interested initially) – you want them to associate each other with good things, not shouting or telling off, or a chase or fight. You can feed the cats in the same room and move them gradually closer together, again getting them used to each other's calm company.

When you feel that it is time to let them out together, then withhold food so that both cats are hungry. Choose a room where there are plenty of hiding places and high shelves or furniture that the cats might use to get off the ground. Put the cat's food down and let the new cat out – don't try and get them too close initially. Keep a watchful eye – they are likely to try and hide from each other at first. You can then gradually let them into the rest of the house when you feel the time is right.

This all sounds very easy. However, few cats will simply then curl up with each other and become bosom buddies. Most will take weeks or months (and even sometimes years) to relax with each other. It is usually easier with kittens and they may become quite close; however, bringing in a new adult cat will probably be more difficult, and the best you may be able to hope for is that they tolerate each other in the same room. Every cat is different and the way it reacts will depend on its personality and previous experiences of mixing with other cats – it will also, of course, depend on the new cat. If it is fairly quiet and lives alongside the original pet in a peaceful manner, then things will probably settle easily. If it is a bully or a cat that itself does not want to share a feline home, then it may be more difficult, both for the resident cat and for you!

## TOO MANY CATS?

Adding cats to a household can be very easy – for people, that is. It may not be so straightforward from the cat's point of view. They all look great draped over the furniture; you love them all individually and you can cram quite a few into an average house. Collecting cats can become addictive. In chapter 11 the point was made that cats which are stressed will often internalize their problems – they will become quiet; they will huddle away; they will stay outside or remain hidden under the bed. You can get away with putting quite a lot of stress on some cats before you get any visible signs or reactions. Of course, some people seem to be able to keep about 10 cats together without any of them seeming to be the least concerned. However, for the rest of us mere mortals, it is often a mistake to keep more than three cats. At this level, something almost inevitably grates on one of them and you may get behavioral problems. I am not basing this statement on research findings – it is borne of listening to problems and talking to owners over many years. Know when you have enough and don't upset the apple cart if the situation is happy already! Most behaviorists only keep one or two cats.

And it is not just in our homes that large densities of cats can cause a problem – some urban areas have huge numbers of cats living very close together. This too can cause problems for cats.

# INDOOR-ONLY CATS

Throughout this book I refer to indoor cats and by these I mean cats that are not allowed outside at all. Their owners may keep them inside because they live close to a road or in an area that is dangerous for cats to go out in. Sometimes owners just want to keep their cats safe from all danger and keep them in despite living in a relatively safe place. Safety is one of the things we want for our cats, and it may be the cause of some problems because the cats themselves do not appreciate the limitations it places upon them. Of course, if you want to have an indoor cat, you cannot simply take one that is used to going out and keep it in. Most cats will be very upset by this and will spend a great deal of time trying to escape from the household; they may develop behavioral problems because they feel frustrated at being confined.

Living in the middle of nowhere in the countryside I am in a privileged position to talk about how cats are kept. My own cats can roam with relative safety and there are few other cats in the vicinity. I realize I am lucky to be able to do this. I have lost cats because they have been run over or through unforeseen accidents, but I feel that the quality and richness of their outdoor lives is a match for the risks. As I watch my cats in the yard and going about their very independent lives, I have no regrets. I also have lots of open windows and children who would never remember to keep doors closed – to have to keep on telling the children to shut them would introduce another stress factor for the whole family!

Many people who keep cats indoors will say their pets are perfectly happy. They may be so – cats vary hugely in their personalities and some may not even want to go out. Nervous cats especially may choose to stay indoors rather than face the threats they perceive to be outdoors – they make excellent indoor cats. Other cats are just naturally going to want more, and these are the ones to worry about. Owners can do a great deal to keep their indoor cats stimulated. Remember that cats typically eat between 7 and 20 small snacks a day. If they were not fed by people, they would have to catch all of these. Researchers say that only 1 in 15 hunting episodes is successful, so to catch even 10 small meals, a cat will have to try 150 times – that means a lot of activity. Hunting behavior can be driven by hunger, but it can also be carried out independently: cats almost automatically react to movement or sound as their instincts drive them to keep hunting. This is a lot of activity to miss out on for the indoor cat, especially at the young stage of around one year old. Cats with access to the outdoors and that hunt will be pretty prolific at this age, and up until about three years old, when hunting activities seem to tail off a little (although some cats keep going at a higher level throughout their lives). The young indoor cat may become bored or frustrated if its owners are not giving it a level of play or mock hunting to satisfy this outlet of energy. We all know that our dogs need to be walked in order to exercise them and let them.enjoy running free and investigating smells. If we do not, we know that they will have lots of pent-up energy and may become destructive or even aggressive because they have not worked off the need to do something. Likewise, teachers know that if young children have to be kept in the classroom over lunch or break time because it is raining, they may be more fidgety in the afternoon. Many of them need to go out and run to move around and burn up some energy. We do not seem to think the same way about our cats. Because they tend to lie around and sleep when they are indoors, we think that they are happy doing this. They probably are if they have spent several hours patrolling the yard or hunting. Cats need stimulation and exercise, too.

Owners of indoor cats (especially young ones) need to be playing with them a great deal (remember: 150 hunting trips!) and providing new things for them to climb into and onto and investigate. There is probably a case for environmental enrichment, as is provided for animals in zoos – letting the cats find their food hidden around the house, for example. In this way their minds are kept active and they get to "hunt" for their food. Indeed, some breeders have been providing large exercise wheels for their cats – along the lines of those used by hamsters. Apparently the cats love them – it certainly gives them a chance to burn off some energy.

Some very active and sociable cats such as Siamese can become very attached, indeed over-attached, to their owners in these circumstances. They sleep when their owners are not around, and when they are present, they become very demanding and very dependent upon them. Some people like this intensity of relationship and if the owner has nothing else to do, then perhaps it is quite mutually rewarding. However, if the owner has other things to do, such as work or the enjoyment of a social life, the cat can become very upset when the owner is not there. When the owner is there, the cat is totally demanding – as one friend put it, "The cat does not have an alternative life of its own, so it takes over the owner's." These cats may start to undertake displacement activities in an attempt to calm themselves when the owner is away – a common activity in these circumstances is overgrooming. At first the cat grooms as a normal part of its everyday behavior and to relieve tension. However, this does not relieve all the tension, because much of it is caused by the absence of the owner. It grooms more in an attempt to put the situation right, and it becomes an obsession. Often these cats have bald patches where they have licked off all the hair.

Another problem that occurs with active cats kept indoors is redirected aggression. They see another cat, or are stimulated by birds, or movement out of the window. Their system automatically gets ready to fight or hunt. However, there is no outlet for this behavior and the cat becomes frustrated. Owners of such cats remark that on certain occasions, they were simply walking by when the cat attacked them – sometimes quite nastily. The aroused cat has focused on something moving and pounced. Perhaps because most activity is already focused on the owner, it makes sense to aim the aggression in that direction, too. Some of these cats also start to control their owners by preventing them from getting up the stairs, or into a certain room, by being aggressive.

The therapy for such cats is to give them something to interest them aside from their owner – to tire them out with play and to make their lives fuller. Sometimes this can involve getting another cat – bearing in mind that it can be very difficult to introduce a new cat into the territory of a totally indoor cat because it is a total violation of its space, and it has nowhere to escape to, such as out into the yard. It is not used to dealing with new scents and new situations because its life is totally controlled by its owner, so changes may become difficult. Introductions must be done very carefully (and this is the reason it is suggested that indoor cats should come in pairs).

Some cats can become very sensitive to changes in the household, such as new furniture, or even just new items of clothing, or even black plastic bags, and can be upset at their presence. One such indoor cat began spraying indoors because its owner brought her bicycle, which she rode to work on every day, into the hall at night. Of course, she had driven through all sorts of smells on the way and had brought them into the cat's safe household.

Rather than try not to upset the cat by keeping everything the same, it is better to desensitize it by adding novelty and helping the cat to get a life of its own. If the owner happens to have a yard (which may not be safe to let the cat out in, as it might escape), fencing it in is an excellent option. By building high, metal fencing that overhangs at the top and putting collars on any trees the cat could use to scale, the yard can be made escape-proof. The cat can then have a whole new world open up before it. Owners of houses without yards or apartments above the ground floor will have to work extra hard inside with their cats. Some owners have actually built cat rooms with lots of different shelves, cat entertainment climbing centers, ropes, and so forth to keep their cats amused. If you compare it to keeping an animal in the zoo, the owners are the environmental enrichment when they are around, but they have to ensure that the cats have some interest and challenges when they are out, too. Owners have to live in their cat's environment. Luckily, human comforts such as beds and soft furnishings are also considered feline luxuries.

## BRINGING OUTDOOR BEHAVIORS INSIDE

We are very happy for our cats to scratch or spray, urinate or defecate outdoors. For many cats, these behaviors go on outside the sphere of their owners and often some or all of them go unnoticed by their owners. It is only when the cats start to carry out these natural behaviors in the wrong place – i.e., indoors – that owners begin to think that there might be a problem. A behavioral problem in a cat is usually a natural behavior taking place in the wrong place. Occasionally, as in overgrooming, it is a natural behavior that is taken to excess.

When a cat starts to mark more indoors, either scratching more or spraying, it is a sign that it is feeling under threat or insecure about something and that it is trying to make its indoor territory feel more secure. Some of the things that can make a cat feel insecure are:

Other cats outdoors becoming threatening, coming near or even into the house.
A new cat in the house.
Building or alteration work that upsets the household.
Decoration or new furniture.
A new person in the house.
A new baby in the house.
All of these may threaten the cat's feeling of safety. It is up to owners to try and "think cat," to find the cause and alter it if possible, while also making the cat feel more secure. Feelings of security can be improved by:

Locking the cat flap if other cats are coming in, or letting the cat in and out while chasing other cats out of the yard.
Using a water pistol to discourage other cats from hanging around in the yard or near the cat flap.
Giving the cat high areas around the house for retreat to get away from other cats, dogs, or children.
Giving the cat a regular lifestyle – for example, timing the cat's feeding – so that it knows just what is going to happen and when.

If the cat is urinating or soiling in the wrong place, it could be due to a mixture of security problems and housekeeping problems. This can be improved by:

Making sure the litter is of a type the cat likes.
Making sure the litter tray is kept clean enough.
Putting a cover over the tray in case the cat feels vulnerable.
Making sure the cat has access to the tray at all times and is not annoyed by children, dogs, or other cats when using it.
Putting the tray in a place where the cat feels safe.

## CHANGES IN BEHAVIOR IN CATS

Sometimes owners become worried because, for example, their seven-year-old cat has suddenly begun to hiss and spit occasionally if they go near it. While they can see no obvious explanation or threat that could have brought on the behavior, they are worried about their cat. In these circumstances, it is wise to have the cat checked over by the vet. Illness can cause changes in behavior by changing the chemistry of the body. Changes in behavior can also result from pain or feeling unwell or confused – all of which makes the cat feel vulnerable. When I read the explanation of a "field of aggression" in cats, a lot of feline behavior falls into place. How can a cat be perfectly friendly in one place or one situation and be unapproachable only a short time later? To recap on our earlier discussion of this topic, the "field of aggression" theory argues that when the cat is relaxed and happy with the world, its field of aggression is smaller than its body – people can approach it and it will be friendly and calm. However, as the cat becomes stressed, tension builds, or it feels threatened, its field of aggression grows –

anything that comes within this area around it is likely to be reacted to with defensive aggression. Thus, if the cat is feeling very stressed because it is ill or it knows there is another cat in the vicinity that may appear at any time, it will react accordingly – the field may have a circumference of a couple of yards.

This may explain how cats can switch moods very quickly and sometimes seemingly without reason – a threat needs to be reacted to quickly, and when the body goes into defensive mode, anything nearby may be considered threatening.

Some cats will "switch" from one behavior to another with a certain cat, but then never switch back. Several owners have described a scenario to me that occurred when they stood on the tail of one of a pair of cats they owned (by accident); the cat made that feline yowl of surprise and pain and the second cat, who happened to be close by, attacked the first cat, much to its surprise. Sometimes these had been cats that had lived together in apparent harmony for many years. However, once the episode and attack had occurred, they never got along again. A similar thing has been reported in cats when one of a pair goes to the veterinarian and presumably comes back smelling of the office. The cat that stayed at home reacts to it, hissing and growling. The cats may never get along again as they used to, or it may take quite some time to get them to feel relaxed with each other again. I don't think we understand feline psychology enough to explain these episodes in which one small incident can negate years of harmonious cohabitation. It may illustrate the relative importance (or not) of other feline relationships to cats. Perhaps this is another of these feline enigmas and no doubt there is a biochemical explanation. We still need a few more years of study in this area to be able to establish exactly what it is.

# PHEROMONES – A USEFUL TOOL

If you have waded your way through this book, by this point you will be well aware of the power of scent for cats and be familiar with pheromones – chemicals that the cat produces which it uses to leave scent messages for itself and for other cats. They have a range of meanings depending on the context in which they are used. When cats are feeling under threat, they often resort to increased marking activities – leaving more scents of various types around to try and feel secure. Just recently researchers have been able to synthetically produce some parts (or fractions) of the scents produced by the glands on the face, and they have been using them in different situations to see what effect they have on the cat's behavior. Cat facial secretions may contain up to 40 chemicals. Thirteen of these are common to all cats and apparently no cat secretes all the chemicals at the same time. This would seem to give the cat plenty of scope for producing many and various types of scent. Workers have found five "functional fractions" (numbered F1–F5) for which they think there are distinct roles. Two of these, F3 and F4, can now be made artificially. The F3 fraction is available commercially as Feliway (made by Ceva Animal Health and available from veterinarians). Studies have shown that using this scent in homes where cats are spraying can reduce the spraying behavior considerably. It worked with spraying induced by stress, but not by sexual arousal. The pheromones do not work so well where there is actual aggression between cats in the household, which may point to the pheromones being a form of passive aggression in a situation of threat that has not escalated to aggression. Once physical violence is in the equation, there also needs to be some form of behavioral therapy to try and resolve the problem.

The synthetic pheromone has also been used to reduce stress when traveling, by being sprayed into the cat carrier half an hour before traveling; it also seems to help in the veterinary office and will relax cats and allow treatment more easily. The cats seem to be able to deal with stress better and it may be useful to help cats recovering from surgery or illness in this way. Sprayed on furniture which is scratched, it resulted in cats finding somewhere else to scratch – a redirection of the behavior rather than a suppression.

The manufacturers have recently produced the product in the form of a plug-in diffuser – the type which is used to freshen rooms by providing a continual release of scent. This too seems to have been successful in reducing spraying behaviors.

The F4 fraction (Felifriend) has been found to encourage animals to approach unfamiliar people and adapt to a new environment, and may be useful in introducing cats to a new person or a new house.

## HELP IN THE VETERINARY OFFICE

Some forward-thinking veterinary hospitals and offices are taking what we know about cat behavior and how cats react in a stressful situation and applying it to the cats in their care. The sick cat is already trying to deal with a medical problem, so it may be feeling pretty stressed already. It then has to go into the veterinary office for an operation or an examination – add another stress level. The stressed cat may also stop eating. What could be worse for a body that is in trouble than to remove its fuel? It is forced to break down its own tissues to fuel the work of breathing, heating, moving, and all those other activities the body undertakes. Veterinarians know that the sooner you can get an animal or a person to eat after a procedure or operation (before which they have usually been starved anyway), the faster it will recover. Granny's chicken soup is very necessary to build up strength and help recovery.

One of the first things these veterinary hospitals or offices do is to ensure the cats are separated from the dogs. Imagine having an operation and waking to find you are surrounded by members of a different species that you may well have had bad experiences with in the past. They will certainly feel very threatening – could you relax to sleep or eat? Separating cats from dogs allows the cats to relax.

Veterinarians at prominent veterinary schools with feline units have found that the cats there start to eat and therefore recover more quickly if they undertake a few simple tasks:

Separate cats from dogs.
Give the cats a cardboard box to hide in (lined with nice, warm bedding, of course).
If cats are very nervous or agitated, cover the front of the cage with a blanket so the cats can hide.
Spray inside the cage with Feliway.
Give more nervous cats a higher cage so they feel safer.

Veterinarians at these feline units have found that the cats soon snuggle in and start to knead their bedding and begin to eat once they feel happier. This makes their recovery much more rapid, since the body can start rebuilding itself much more easily.

## CONCLUSION

Part of the fascination of cats is their mystery. We still don't understand why they do all of the things that they do. They live alongside us so successfully that we almost take them for granted.

Most of the time we get away with this because they get on with their lives while we get on with ours. We interact and enjoy the interaction when either side feels the need. However, on occasion we need to be alert to the needs of our cats because they are feeling stressed or distressed. We have to get to know our own cats – whether they like interaction with us; whether they prefer not to be given attention; whether they need full attention all the time; whether they are confident outside as well as in – and so it goes on. If we keep cats in a way in which they have little chance of having some control over their lives, such as indoors, then we have to work at the situation – like the mandatory walking of a dog, we must play with the cats and make time to entertain them and keep them agile in mind and body. If our cats are distressed by things going on outside, then we need to be able to try and help them. If we want to take on more cats, we must be aware of the resultant stress on our original cat or cats. If we are aware of the experiences necessary to kittens to make them able to cope with the human world, then we must ensure that they get this exposure at the right time and in the right amounts. All of these things can make a great deal of difference toward how content our cats are. It can be difficult to notice if they are only mildly stressed – they tend to keep quiet or run away if they can. Veterinarians who are involved with pain control in animals find cats very difficult subjects, as it can be almost impossible to ascertain when they are in pain – they cover it well. Only when they start to exhibit obvious behavioral changes do we get the message. Luckily, many owners are finely tuned to their cats and their sixth sense tells them that something is not right. Learning more about our feline companions' normal behaviors and motivations may help us to understand them when they are in distress.

Don't take cats for granted; they are fantastic creatures of poise, elegance, and intelligence. We need to admire them for the animals they are and not try and anthropomorphize their behaviors. The relationship between humans and cats has been one of the most successful love stories over the years. A successful relationship needs respect and an ability to give both sides a chance to express their own personalities. Cats have long fitted in with us – we have to make sure that we do not try and change them to fit human needs, but admire them instead for their natural and wonderful feline ways.